BLOOMSBURY

BLOOMSBURY

QUENTIN BELL

NEW EDITION

WEIDENFELD & NICOLSON
LONDON

C. M. 1899–1966

Reprinted 1990
First published in Great Britain by
George Weidenfeld & Nicolson Limited
91 Clapham High Street
London SW4

ISBN 0 297 78826 4 Paperback

Printed by Butler & Tanner Ltd, Frome and London

Contents

Foreword to the New Edition

In 1967 John Gross approached me on behalf of Weidenfeld & Nicolson with the idea of a book on the Pre-Raphaelites. Being already embarked on a similar project and having just begun my biography of Virginia Woolf I suggested Bloomsbury as an alternative subject. John accepted the idea. In doing this he showed characteristic courage.

In 1967 there were many good reasons for not writing about Bloomsbury and some even better ones for not employing me to do the job. Bloomsbury at that time seemed dead and stinking. It seemed dead inasmuch as the few survivors had for long been out of fashion and the rest dismissed by a subsequent generation of critics. It stank in the noses of all good journalists who could hardly allude to it without using their pocket handkerchiefs. Of the individuals who composed the group only Maynard Keynes enjoyed some favour with the public.

Since *Bloomsbury*'s original publication the more celebrated members of the group have been examined in detail by a succession of expert authors and no longer do they need me to defend them. I hope, however, that in this book I have been able to give a fairly useful impression of the group and an account of the reasons why it aroused such very varying emotions.

Quentin Bell
Sussex, 1985

1

Introductory

It is necessary that I should begin by saying a few words about myself. I was born and bred in Bloomsbury; writing about it I must write about my friends and relations. As an historian I have, therefore, certain advantages and disadvantages; I write with some personal knowledge of my subject, I can regard myself as a 'primary source', although it must be borne in mind that my own recollections are confined to the last phase of Bloomsbury's existence. On the other hand, in addressing myself to a subject which of its very nature presents formidable difficulties, I have the further disadvantage of discussing a topic which involves my affections. The historian who does this is likely to be accused of partiality; his honesty is put to the test and, even though he may acquit himself before the bar of his own conscience, he may still be guilty of some offences unknown to that court.

Let me therefore examine two charges, one of which involves a conscious, the other an unconscious offence. To the first I must plead guilty. I have omitted a good deal that I know and much more at which I can guess concerning the private lives of the people whom I shall discuss. This is, primarily, a study in the history of ideas, and although the *mœurs* of Bloomsbury have to be considered and will in a general way be described, I am not required nor am I inclined to act as Clio's chambermaid, to sniff into commodes or under beds, to open love-letters or to scrutinise diaries. On the present occasion I shall leave Bloomsbury linen, whether clean or dirty, unaired.

The nature of my unconscious offences, if there are any, may best be described by referring to Mr Roy Harrod's *Life of John Maynard Keynes*. Harrod describes a manner of speech – a use of cadence – which derives from Lytton Strachey and which, he says, was universal in Bloomsbury, Maynard Keynes himself being the solitary exception. I find this hard to believe; Lytton

Strachey undoubtedly had a very special way of talking and most of his family spoke in rather the same manner; but to me it seems that no one who was not a Strachey ever spoke like a Strachey. My incredulity proves very little; brought up with the accents of Bloomsbury continually in my ears I should, naturally, be deaf to their peculiarities. No doubt I too speak in this manner. It is, I must confess, a painful thought; but Harrod is a fair and a sympathetic observer; he may be right. If he is, then clearly it is possible that I may at an early age have contracted some moral habits, some intellectual body odour which may be as infectious and as hard to detect in one's own person as are fashions of speech. To this charge, clearly, I can make no plea.

Bloomsbury was always under fire. This is the common fate of all groups, coteries and cliques, particularly if they have sufficient liveliness to make a new contribution to the thought of their time. If that contribution has been connected with the arts, then contemporary reactions are likely to be very hostile and the aftermath of success is likely to be depreciation. Art lives by destroying itself and, as fashions change, artists and their works grow, fade, and sometimes grow again in public estimation. Bloomsbury certainly has not been exempt from these variations of aesthetic feeling and today its situation is not unlike that of the Pre-Raphaelites forty years ago. Bloomsbury however was unlike the Pre-Raphaelites in that it has been criticised from a bewilderingly large number of points of view.

Let me take two examples, for they will help the reader to understand some of the difficulties that arise when one attempts to talk about Bloomsbury, and will lead us, I hope, to a method of discussion which will give us some notion of its true character.

Mr A.D. Moody tells us that Bloomsbury was a sub-group of the intellectual élite:

> 'They had the requisite residue of Hebraic conscience, expressed mostly in righteous scorn for the barbarian, philistine and populace, to which all outsiders were consigned; and they subscribed to the Greek heritage. Since their concern was all

> for the civilisation in the mind, they regarded as outsiders the main body of the establishment who were concerned with the more practical problems of governing and civilising.'[1]

This is very different from the view expressed by Professor John Jewkes in *Ordeal by Planning.* If Bloomsbury had confined itself to the 'civilisation in the mind', if it had dissociated itself from practical problems of governing and civilising, he might not have disapproved of it so strongly. Its role, in his view, was to 'stimulate, energise, verbalise and organise the general hostile atmosphere which surrounds the capitalist engine.' Bloomsbury was composed of 'the scribblers of the left . . . men who . . . by their lack of wisdom and their malicious desire to upset have acted as a continually destabilising social influence.'[2]

Professor Jewkes is not alone in his opinions nor, certainly, is Mr Moody the only critic to see in Bloomsbury something precious, remote, and upper class. These variations of opinion result, to a great extent, from the different manners in which Bloomsbury has been defined. And this, obviously, is a matter of crucial importance, all the more so because 'membership' of Bloomsbury may be regarded not simply as a matter of intellectual affinity but of moral responsibility. In *Modern English Painters* Sir John Rothenstein takes the view that Bloomsbury was not so much an artistic as a criminal association. He writes thus:

> 'I doubt . . . whether more than a few people are even now aware how closely-knit an association "Bloomsbury" was, how untiring its members were in advertising one another's work and personalities . . . They would have been surprised if they had known of the lengths to which some of these people – . . . with their gentle Cambridge voices, their informal manners, their casual unassuming clothes, their civilized personal relations with one another – were prepared to go in order to ruin, utterly, not only the "reactionary" figures whom they publicly denounced, but young painters and writers who showed themselves too independent to come to terms with the canons observed by "Bloomsbury", or, more precisely, with the current "party line" which varied from month to month in accordance

> with what their leader considered the most "significant" trends of opinion prevailing in Paris. If such independence was allied to gifts of an order to provoke rivalry, then so much the worse for the artists. And bad for them it *was*, for there was nothing in the way of slander and intrigue to which certain of the "Bloomsburys" were not willing to descend. I rarely knew hatreds pursued with so much malevolence over so many years; against them neither age nor misfortune offered the slightest protection.'[3]

Because this passage appears in a book which contains valuable information, because it has been reprinted, unaltered, and has been accepted without doubt or qualification by at least one credulous scholar, it is necessary to point out that the author of this philippic has been challenged to show evidence that will tend to justify his assertions and, after ten years, has still failed to do so. No one who knew Bloomsbury at all well, whether they liked or disliked it, will accept this picture of an intellectual *mafia* and, as our knowledge of the period increases, this remarkable outburst will presumably appear increasingly nonsensical. It has however a certain interest. The author is surely sincere, writing as he does with the generous though injudicious enthusiasm of a friend; his remarks form a preface to his study of Wyndham Lewis, who believed that he had indeed been persecuted by Bloomsbury. I discuss these transactions later; but here I want rather to consider the circumstances that make these and other criticisms so easy and, almost inevitably, so misleading.

Sir John writes about Bloomsbury as though it were the Communist Party, the Society of Jesus or the Carbonari, a 'closely-knit association' with canons, a party line and a leader. In fact it was less organised, less ideologically homogeneous than the Pre-Raphaelite Brotherhood, the 'Souls' or even the Impressionists. It had no form of membership, no rules, no leaders; it can hardly be said to have had any common ideas about art, literature or politics, and although it had, I believe, a common attitude to life and was united by friendships, it was as amorphous a body as a group of friends can be.

As a natural consequence it is possible to criticise Bloomsbury

Woodcut by Dora Carrington for 'The Mark on the Wall', Virginia Woolf's contribution to *Two Stories*, the first publication of the Hogarth Press, 1917

as one pleases so long as one defines it in a convenient way. Mr Moody might legitimately claim that Desmond MacCarthy, Clive Bell and Duncan Grant were not greatly concerned with the practical problems of governing and civilising but he disregards Maynard Keynes and Leonard Woolf. One could accommodate Keynes and Woolf within Professor Jewkes's description; but not the other members of the group.

There is moreover this to be remembered: an anonymous group is not only easier to attack than is an individual; it is also much easier to hate. Sir John Rothenstein, affable, courteous and urbane in all his dealings with individual members of Bloomsbury, is nevertheless able to fabricate a fearful fiend, a corporate being of almost unimaginable wickedness. Thus Bloomsbury is always fair game because it can stand for whatever prey the sportsman wishes to kill and easy game because he can 'fire into the brown'.

The question remains, why should it be chosen as a target? I hope presently to find some answers.

What then was Bloomsbury? It is obviously necessary that I should give some kind of answer to this question, yet to me it is clear that no completely satisfactory answer is possible. Those who, by my definition, stood at the centre of Bloomsbury differ amongst themselves. Clive Bell doubts even whether it ever existed. Under the circumstances commentators who stood outside the group may be pardoned for being a little vague. Mr Moody makes no mention of Roger Fry, Duncan Grant or E. M. Forster; Mr Johnstone, while including Forster and Fry, says nothing about Maynard Keynes. Mr Swinnerton includes Lord Russell; Mr Harrod mentions names I have barely heard of. All I can do is to say who was, in my opinion, certainly Bloomsbury, who stood very near to Bloomsbury, and to mention certain principles which can I think be applied, very broadly, in determining who was and who was not Bloomsbury.

The Memoir Club, which was formed in 1920, may furnish an indication. Among its original members were Clive and Vanessa Bell, Lytton Strachey, Leonard and Virginia Woolf, Desmond and Molly MacCarthy, Duncan Grant, E. M. Forster, Roger Fry, Maynard Keynes. In this society the members read their memoirs aloud and clearly it was necessary that a high degree of confident intimacy should obtain amongst them. I should say therefore that all these might be regarded as being 'Bloomsbury', although the MacCarthys and E. M. Forster would probably have said that while very close to Bloomsbury they were not exactly of it. Seeing that Virginia Woolf and Maynard Keynes were also

'The Tub' by Duncan Grant from *Original Woodcuts by Various Artists*, Omega Workshops, 1918

capable of denying that they were actually 'members' and seeing that there was no such thing, properly speaking, as 'membership' it is hard to know how much importance to attach to such disclaimers. At least membership of the Memoir Club in its early days gives one a clue.

If the club had been formed in the year 1913 it would probably have included some other names: Adrian Stephen, Saxon Sydney Turner, Gerald Shove perhaps and H. T. J. Norton.

If the Memoir Club provides one guide, another is supplied by the generations. Already before the war the older members were joined by a rather younger generation, notably David Garnett and Francis Birrell: both of these are, as one may say, 'marginal'. During and after the war a great many other people became closely connected with Bloomsbury, but here the difference of age and background is so great that to include them would involve an impossibly wide definition.

Perhaps my idea of Bloomsbury may best be conveyed by means of a diagram. I have tried to give a notion of the sort of pattern that existed in the year 1913.

E. M. Forster

David Garnett

Molly MacCarthy
Sydney Waterlow Desmond MacCarthy

Roger Fry
Vanessa Bell
Duncan Grant Virginia Woolf
Clive Bell Saxon Sydney Turner
Leonard Woolf
Lytton Strachey Adrian Stephen
Maynard Keynes

Gerald Shove

James Strachey H. T. J. Norton
Marjorie Strachey

Francis Birrell

I have wondered whether I should append biographical notes. It hardly seems likely that the reader will want to be told that Morgan Forster is the author of *A Passage to India* or that Roger Fry brought Post-Impressionism to England and, to quote from the *Concise Dictionary of National Biography*, 'established a position as a critic which made him the greatest influence on taste since Ruskin.' He will surely have heard of Maynard Keynes, Lytton Strachey and Virginia Woolf, or he would not be reading this book. Perhaps he should be reminded that Clive Bell was an important art critic and theorist of Post-Impressionism, that Duncan Grant was certainly the best-known British painter of his generation between the wars, that Desmond MacCarthy was a dramatic and literary critic, that James Strachey was a psycho-analyst and Freud's editor in this country, that David Garnett is a writer, and that Leonard Woolf is an author, publisher and politician.

The biographical notes become more necessary when one ventures beyond this startling constellation of talents. The paintings of Vanessa Bell are known to a comparatively small circle of amateurs. Francis Birrell, the son of Augustine Birrell, died in 1935; he left no considerable monument outside the memory of a large number of devoted friends. The same may be said of Molly MacCarthy. Norton, a gifted mathematician, died unknown; the name of Gerald Shove is known mainly to economists, that of Adrian Stephen to psycho-analysts. Sydney Waterlow was a diplomat. Marjorie Strachey was a teacher of genius but she had none of her brother's talent for writing; Saxon Sydney Turner – an impressive figure at Cambridge – retreated in early life into the Treasury and disappeared, so far as he was able to do so, from the world. To these names we should perhaps add one which is not on my diagram. Thoby Stephen died in 1906, before Bloomsbury was properly in existence. For his sisters at all events he was and remained an all-important figure, silent yet central, like Percival in *The Waves*.

In these pages I must necessarily devote my attention to those of the group who have written their names high and large upon the walls of history; to look at the others is beyond my power and beyond the scope of this book. Nevertheless their existence should

1 Leslie Stephen, father of Vanessa, Thoby, Virginia and Adrian Stephen

2 Leslie Stephen with his second wife Julia at St Ives; in the background their younger daughter Virginia

3 & 4 Sir Richard and Lady Strachey, the parents of Lytton, Marjorie, James and seven other children

5 & 6 Sir Edward and Lady Fry, Roger Fry's parents

7 & 8 Florence and Neville Keynes, parents of Maynard Keynes

9 Gordon Square, Bloomsbury. Here in 1904 the four orphaned children of Leslie Stephen made their home; their example was to be followed by many of their friends

not be forgotten. The influence of Adrian Stephen on his sister Virginia Woolf, or of Saxon Sydney Turner upon his contemporaries must have been considerable; some day it will, perhaps, be described.

The existence of this more or less unknown element in Bloomsbury is but one more complexity in a task which was already sufficiently complex. My diagram is, as I have said, inexact; it may be likened to an attempt to fix the dimensions of a whirlpool, to assess the character of a beast that is half chameleon and half hydra. And this volatile irregular entity must for convenience' sake be personified and called Bloomsbury. Nothing could be more inexact or more irritating. Let me give an example of the kind of difficulty that occurs.

In a recent broadcast biography of Constant Lambert one of the speakers, discussing Lambert's success in the 1920s, said (I quote from memory, but not, I think, inaccurately): 'Even the pundits of Bloomsbury were ready to praise him.' This was followed by a quotation from Maynard Keynes. The inference here is that Bloomsbury had some uniform principle of musical taste which one would not expect to be favourable to Lambert.

Now a certain number of the people to whom I have referred were musically educated (Maynard Keynes, as it happens, was not one of them) but to suppose that Bloomsbury had a hard-and-fast musical doctrine would be about as sensible as it would be to assert that there was a Bloomsbury view of ornithology, ballistics or gardening. How misleading such phrases may be would I think be clear if I were to apply the broadcaster's method in another direction and, considering Maynard Keynes as an economist rather than as a music critic (a not unjustifiable proceeding), I were to point out that Bloomsbury's views of credit, currency and full employment now dominate the economic thinking of the Western world, that we live in an era of Bloomsbury capitalism regulated by Bloomsbury banking and Bloomsbury tax structures. The absurdity of such propositions hardly needs to be pointed out, but it is no more absurd than the notion that Bloomsbury had a collective musical doctrine.

I hope that I may avoid this kind of loose thinking but undoubtedly I shall have to furnish Bloomsbury with a volition, a state of mind, attitudes and appetites. The reader should allow for the fact that, in so doing, I am merely indicating the tendencies of thought and feeling which were to some extent characteristic of the majority of these very distinct and peculiar personalities.

2

Bloomsbury before 1914

Bloomsbury was begotten in Cambridge at the beginning of the century. To be more exact it started at Trinity College during the autumn of 1899. At that time student friendships and student societies brought most of the men in the group together. Leonard Woolf, Lytton Strachey, Saxon Sydney Turner – all members of the 'Apostles' Society – met Thoby Stephen and Clive Bell at the Midnight Society; Desmond MacCarthy came earlier, Maynard Keynes later; Roger Fry had already left Cambridge and did not join the rest until 1910.

Like most Cambridge undergraduates at that time they came from middle-class homes and from a variety of cultural backgrounds. But two of them, Thoby Stephen and Lytton Strachey, clearly belonged by birth to what has been called the 'intellectual aristocracy' of London, and this, by reason of its relationship to Cambridge and because of its connection with members of the group who were to become important at a later stage, is of some importance when one considers the intellectual ancestry of Bloomsbury. Leonard Woolf, coming from a Jewish home in Lexham Gardens, and Clive Bell, from a family which drew its wealth from Welsh mines and expended it upon the destruction of wild animals, had everything to gain and, apart from their native intelligence, little to contribute to the society in which they found themselves. They were, quite simply, in revolt against the parental influence. For Stephen and for Strachey the situation must have been more complex; in their ancestry one finds a vast, and to me obscure, tangle of family inter-connections and intellectual alliances. Stracheys are connected by marriage to Grants and by close friendship to Ritchies, Ritchies are connected to Thackerays and hence to Stephens; they are also connected by marriage to MacCarthys. Stephens, if one goes far enough back, are connected by religious affiliations to Thorntons and hence to

Forsters. Both Stephens and Stracheys had felt the influence of nineteenth-century agnosticism; they were also connected with the history of Anglo-India and to some extent with that of Cambridge – the Cambridge of Sidgwick, Maitland and Fawcett. For the latest generation, that which came up during the autumn of 1899, Cambridge offered a continuation of the parental tradition.

Cambridge at that time had an enormous amount to give; there had, as Leonard Woolf says, been 'an extraordinary outburst of philosophical brilliance'. M'Taggart, Whitehead, Bertrand Russell and G. E. Moore were all Fellows of Trinity; of these, Russell and Moore were immensely important to the young men, and I imagine they were made even more important by reason of the free intellectual intercourse, the Athenian liberty of speech and speculation, that was offered by 'the Society' – the Apostles.

The great intellectual adventure of the older generation had been concerned with the struggle between faith and reason. The struggle was arduous, and it would be a great mistake to think of our grandfathers as living a sheltered life. Indeed it was the very opposite, for they looked up to Heaven and found that it was a void. Under the circumstances it was perhaps natural that they did not extend their researches to objects nearer home. Leslie Stephen defines their position as well as his own, in the brief notes that he made in 1856 when he had lost his faith in Christianity: 'I now believe in nothing, to put it shortly; but I do not the less believe in morality &c &c. I mean to live and die like a gentleman if possible.' The implication is clear; Stephen might consider that the Christian views concerning the origin and ultimate destiny of men and women were false; but in practice this in no way changed his opinions concerning honourable conduct, and in particular that between ladies and gentlemen.

The co-existence of theological scepticism and moral dogmatism and the manner in which they could, through the operation of a ruthlessly logical mind, come into collision is well illustrated in the case of Fitzjames Stephen, Leslie Stephen's elder brother.

Fitzjames, an Indian civilian and a judge, arrived at what was, substantially, an agnostic position, slowly and reluctantly driven by his own intellectual honesty and a protestant disinclination to accept the idea of spiritual authority; his intellectual weapons, which he uses with the tremendous force of a great lawyer, were forged by Bentham and J. S. Mill. But, unlike most of the Utilitarians, he was a fervent believer in social discipline. This belief was greatly reinforced by the spectacle of authoritarian government in British India, where he met administrators, such as his friend Sir John Strachey, who seemed to him to furnish a pattern of good government. He published his views in a remarkable work, *Liberty, Equality, Fraternity*.

The true end of government, as he saw it, was to enforce morality; morality could only be enforced by coercion. This was not simply a question of expediency. Crime was not to be regarded (as Mill regarded it) as a nuisance; crime was sin. For this reason self-regarding crime – crime, shall we say, between consenting adults – was no less to be chastised than were anti-social offences. Punishments should be inflicted not simply to prevent lawlessness, but to show our hatred of immorality:

> 'Criminal law is in the nature of a persecution of the grosser forms of vice, and an emphatic assertion of the principle that the feeling of hatred and the desire of vengeance . . . (i.e. the emotion, whatever its proper name, produced by the contemplation of vice on healthily constituted minds) are important elements in human nature, which ought in such cases to be satisfied in a regular, public and legal manner.'

This being the nature of the social task, Fitzjames Stephen proceeds, with perfect logic, to consider how it may best be performed and sees that it requires an authoritarian system. The rule of men over women, of monarchs over their subjects, was to be absolute. War was a necessity, and indeed government itself was a form of warfare. The state is justified in suppressing dangerous opinions, and even religious persecution is not impermissible.

'To attack opinions on which the framework of society depends is, and ought to be dangerous. It should be done, if at all, sword in hand.' Religion itself is, at all events, a useful prop for morality and it would certainly be expedient to suppose the existence of 'a Being who, though not wholly benevolent, has so arranged the universe that virtue is the law prescribed to his creatures.' But

God, if He is to act as a deterrent, should be armed with sanctions. Here, for the first time, Stephen wavers; even an English judge may hesitate before pronouncing an eternal sentence, and moreover the belief in Hell was precisely the one theological doctrine which seemed to him completely odious and thoroughly absurd.

It will be seen that Fitzjames Stephen was much nearer in his thought to Carlyle or even to Ruskin than to J. S. Mill. The morality on which he based his reasoning was pretty widely accepted in Victorian England. It was indeed the morality of our criminal code. What Fitzjames did was to point out that such morality implied coercion and that the logical end of Mill's reasoning was either some other morality, or amorality.

Leslie Stephen, in his life of Fitzjames, points out that the great difference between his brother and Mill was one of temperament. 'The two men could never come into cordial relations, and the ultimate reason, I think, was what I should call Mill's want of virility . . . Fitzjames like Henry VIII "loved a man", and the man of Mill's speculations seemed to be a colourless, flaccid creature, who required, before all things, to have some red blood infused into his veins'. 'Mill seemed,' says Leslie Stephen in another place, 'wanting in the fire and force of the full-grown male animal . . . Fitzjames could only make a real friend of a man in whom he could recognise the capacity of masculine emotions.'

Here Leslie Stephen seems to be voicing not only his brother's emotions but his own. It is the kind of statement of which modern biographers tend to be shy. To our minds – they are not perhaps what Fitzjames would have called 'healthily constituted minds' – the love of one man for another man's virility suggests a number of rather awkward speculations, which we need not pursue. I would merely point out that the Victorian idea of virtue involved deep and irrational feeling all the more explosive for being charged with unstable psychological elements, and that this idea remained untouched by the agnosticism of the period.[4]

What this could mean in terms of human relationships we may see in documents of the time; Gosse and Samuel Butler both give us an idea of patriarchal society in the nineteenth century. More to our present purposes is Virginia Woolf's picture of her father in *To the Lighthouse*, and the picture of himself that he gives in a still unpublished account of his married life known by his family as 'The Mausoleum Book'. Drawing on both these sources Noël Annan described the relationship between husband and wife in his life of Leslie Stephen, an account which it would be foolish to paraphrase:

> 'He . . . desired to transform her into an apotheosis of motherhood, but treated her in the home as someone who should be at his beck and call, support him in every emotional crisis, order the minutiae of his life and then submit to his criticism in those household matters of which she was mistress . . . he was for ever trampling upon her feelings, wounding the person who comforted him, half conscious of his hebetude, unable to restrain it.'[5]

And yet, this is not the full picture. Stephen's domestic life after his wife's death, the savage, self-pitying emotional blackmail that he inflicted on his daughters, was something of which they spoke but which they never made public. Virginia Woolf gives no more than a hint of it when she writes of the 'arid scimitar of the male, which smote mercilessly, again and again demanding sympathy.' It is of course possible that she was guilty of exaggeration, and it is the opinion of at least one qualified observer that she was. On the other hand her sister undoubtedly held the same view, while her younger brother felt that Virginia Woolf was altogether too indulgent to their father. Stephen's ruthless self-pity was, at all events, believed in by his children. That he was by his own lights an excellent, indeed an indulgent parent, that he 'lived and died like a gentleman', was something that they would also have conceded. This indeed was the horror of the situation. The boredom, the restriction, the oppression of family life was not the product of individual cruelty but of social habit.

'Girls withering into ladies,' exclaims Shaw's heroine, 'ladies withering into old maids. Nursing old women. Running errands for old men. Good for nothing at last. Oh, you can't imagine the fiendish selfishness of the old people and the maudlin sacrifice of the young.'

This was simply the normal pattern of the middle classes, and where abnormality occurred, when men and women disobeyed the injunctions of social custom, or worse still, when sex wandered in unfamiliar directions, the punishment of the deviant was savage, swift and merciless.

Thus, in Victorian England, we find that the apostles of progress, having swept their churches clean of sacraments, altars, priests and pulpits, leaving nothing save a bare structure of ethical assertions, returned to curtained, cushioned, upholstered homes in which every sort of buried sexual superstition, traditionalist tyranny and emotional cant served as a covering for dirty unswept corners and nameless secular filth.

By 1900 it seemed that the time had come for a re-examination of human emotions. The older generation had proclaimed the importance of seeking the truth, of being wholly and entirely honest about the Pentateuch. Let us not underestimate such an endeavour; there are still plenty of people ready to give crooked answers to the questions of nineteenth-century agnosticism. Still, by the beginning of the twentieth century it seemed proper to put questions of another kind.

The need was for a new honesty and a new charity in personal relations, and I think that everyone in what was to become Bloomsbury felt this, but there were undoubtedly some who also saw the problem in more political terms. The patriarchal family is simply the smallest unit of the patriarchal state; the military and ecclesiastical establishments, the régime of inherited status and the Imperial idea, all rested upon a notion of natural rights and duties which depended in the last analysis upon force and upon traditions of obedience. In so far as young men at Cambridge looked at the outside world they looked for and found a hopeful resurgence of liberal values. In France and even in Germany the forces of clericalism and militarism, of violence and unreason, were challenged as never before. Britain's own imperialist adventures were more and more severely criticised. In a society as sheltered from social storms as England then was, it was easy to be hopeful about the future.

Now, given this predisposition to look for a state of things in which unreason would be replaced by reason and hatred by love – a predisposition which was becoming fairly widespread – one

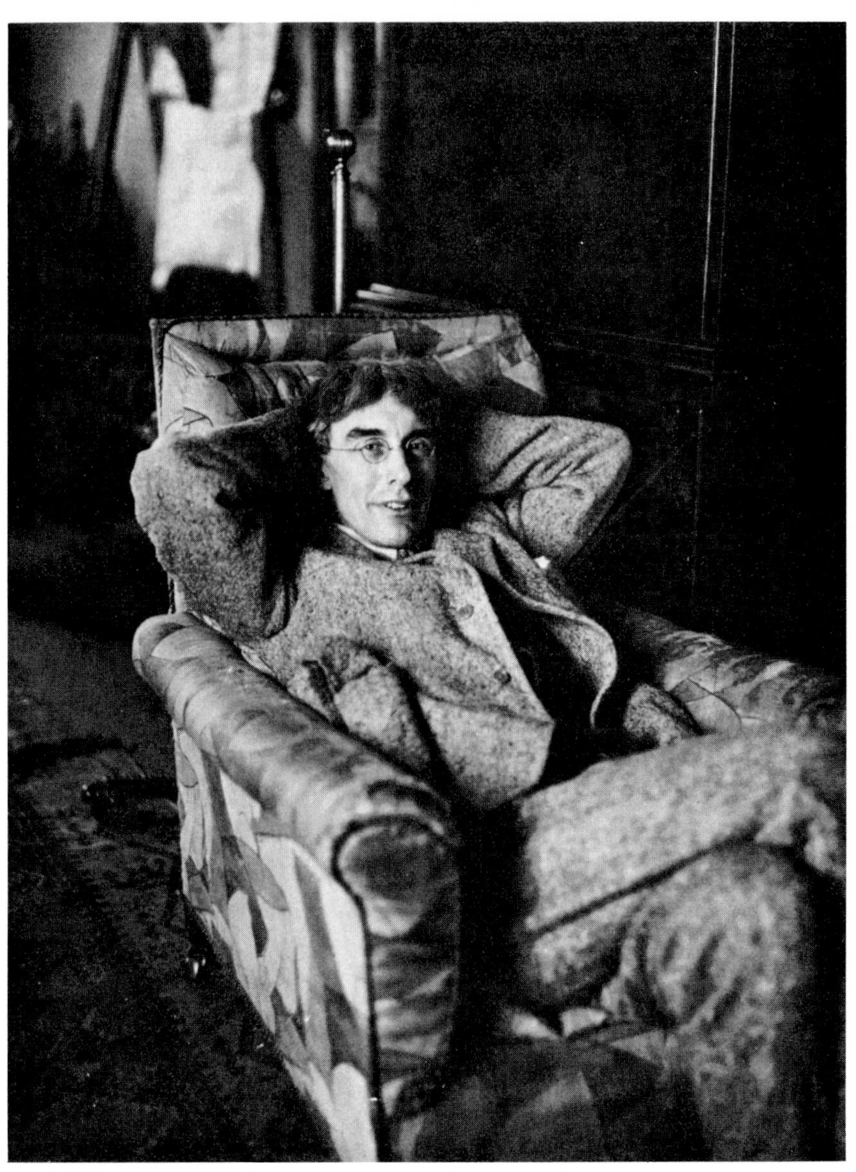

10 Roger Fry, 1918

11 Vanessa Bell, née Stephen, 1907

12 Virginia Stephen, later Woolf, 1907

13 Adrian and Karin Stephen, about the time of their marriage in 1914

14 Thoby Stephen, 1906

15 Saxon Sydney Turner by Vanessa Bell, c. 1908

16 E. M. Forster by Vanessa Bell, 1940

17 Lady Ottoline Morrell by Simon Bussy, c. 1920

18 David Garnett by Vanessa Bell, c. 1916

19 Duncan Grant and Maynard Keynes, c. 1911

might find in the philosophy of G. E. Moore a tremendous instrument of liberation. A morality based, as all legislative moralities must be, on the supposition that certain *acts* are wicked, crumbles if one admits, with Moore, that value resides only in certain states of mind, and a philosophy based upon a belief in the necessity of imposing moral values by the exercise of force can hardly be maintained when it is allowed that all moral questions must be scrutinised in the light of reason, and that the most valuable states of mind are not those that we associate with the hero or even with the saint, but with the contemplation of beauty, love and truth.

Such contemplation, and contemplation with such an end in view, suggests a very passive view of the universe. And yet in its implications, at all events, *Principia Ethica* was a revolutionary work, involving, as Maynard Keynes said, the repudiation of customary morals and conventions and traditional wisdom. Such a combination of pacific method and revolutionary purpose was, I think, one of the characteristics of Bloomsbury.

This tendency of thought, and I cannot claim that it was more than that, was greatly strengthened by the fact that at Cambridge something very like it could be put into practice. Of the young men who formed the nucleus of Bloomsbury, all save Clive Bell and Thoby Stephen were members of that semi-secret Cambridge society The Apostles. What happens when Apostles meet I have but the vaguest idea, but it would seem that, together with a certain gaiety and abandon, there is Moore's first desideratum – a perfect respect for truth and, one supposes, for nothing else. When, under these conditions, the very considerable intellects of Lytton Strachey, Desmond MacCarthy, Saxon Sydney Turner and Leonard Woolf were liberated and licensed it must have seemed that nothing was impossible to the followers of Moore.

Then, in 1903 and 1904, they found their theories confronted by a quite different reality.

Cambridge, like that section of London Society to which Leslie Stephen was attached, valued the intellect above all things. The nineteenth-century Stephens tended to find employment in that eminently intellectual profession, the Bar; they cultivated the

Omega Christmas card, woodcut by Roger Fry, 1913

most cerebral of the arts, the art of literature. They valued 'a hard-headed commonsense that detects humbug and imposture and sentimentalism in many quarters.' I am quoting Maitland, who continues: 'On the possession of this quality Cambridge men, especially the Cambridge men whom Stephen knew best, were wont to pride themselves . . .'. But Stephen himself had married into a different section of London society. Indeed he did so twice, first when he married a Thackeray, then when he married a Jackson.

Let me quote from a letter which Stephen's sister-in-law Annie Thackeray wrote about the year 1870; her method of dating tells us at once how far she was from the strict rationality of Cambridge, for it begins:

'Blois,
Yesterday.

'All the old women have got their white caps on, the east

wind has made every weather-cock shine. I can't think how to tell you what a lovely old place it is, sunny-streaked up and down, stones flung into *now* from St. Louis's days, others rising into carved staircases and gabions and gargoyles. This isn't a description – I wish it were – it isn't white or crisp enough, or high enough. There are broad flights and flights of steps going right up into the air, with the Bishop at the top and the Cathedral Service, and then this wonderful old garden and terrace and castle, and the ghosts of Guise and Henry III looking on through a doorway, and Catherine de Medici in her sunny bedroom opening upon loggias, and old roofs and birds and gardens. It is much more educated and sumptuous than other old towns.'[6]

Do we not hear in these sentences a turn of speech, a volatile kind of thought which hardly reappears in English literature before the publication of *The Voyage Out*? It is a very feminine kind of writing and Lady Ritchie – as she later became – represents what I would describe as a feminine element in the society from which Bloomsbury emerged. She was, incidentally, connected with the Stracheys by friendship and the MacCarthys by marriage as well as with the Stephens. In the continual bickering between her and Leslie Stephen there was a kind of war between sense and sensibility and also between the world of Cambridge and the world of Little Holland House.

Little Holland House, of which the second Mrs Stephen was, as one may say, a child, belonged to her aunt and uncle Mr and Mrs Prinsep, but it was inhabited and visited by artists. Some of these were literary men: Tennyson, Sir Henry Taylor and Thackeray; but Watts was the resident genius, Woolner, Holman Hunt and the Pre-Raphaelites were constant visitors, and above all the place was enlivened by Mrs Cameron (in some ways the most successful of these visual artists) and by her sisters, the beautiful daughters of Mr James Pattle, of whom Mrs Prinsep was one. 'Little Holland House,' wrote Ellen Terry, 'seemed to me a paradise, where only beautiful things were allowed to come. All the women were graceful, and all the men were gifted.' It was undoubtedly the home of a very pleasant society, altogether less intellectual than that of the Stephens, more sentimental, much more concerned with the pleasures of the senses and above all with the pleasures of the visible world.

Leslie Stephen's daughters inherited something from both their very remarkable parents; but their affections lay on the maternal side and although they rejected the aesthetic of Little Holland House they did not reject the assumption that the visual arts were supremely important or – and for Virginia this was of the highest importance – the belief that truth may be apprehended not only by means of ratiocination but by way of intuition and sensibility. This 'un-Cambridge', un-Stephen attitude was perhaps reinforced rather than diminished by their mother's early death (1895) and by the eleven years of their father's widowerhood.

Stephen died in 1904 and his children at once moved from Hyde Park Gate, which was then a good address, to 46 Gordon Square, Bloomsbury, which was not. Their friends thought it a most eccentric, an almost disreputable, proceeding. At about the same time many of Thoby Stephen's Cambridge friends came to London, and naturally enough began to visit him and his sisters.

'These Apostolic young men,' writes Duncan Grant, who, rather later, was introduced to the circle by his cousin Lytton Strachey, 'found to their amazement that they could be shocked by the boldness and scepticism of two young women.'

One would like to know more about this confrontation of the sexes, these meetings on Thursday evenings between the hours of ten and twelve when whiskey, buns and cocoa were provided and talk was free; unfortunately our most trustworthy informant, Leonard Woolf, had sailed away to Ceylon, and what follows is largely guesswork.

Perhaps the essential element in the situation – and that which made it so attractive – was the sense of liberation at 46 Gordon Square. The Stephen children were orphans. They had escaped from an extremely depressing Victorian home. They were young. In that uncontrolled, unchaperoned environment Thoby Stephen's friends might continue the conversation which had begun in Cambridge. Did they, one would like to know, hesitate before doing so?

In their assumption that nothing really matters so long as one is wholehearted in the pursuit of truth they resembled their Victorian predecessors; but to the Victorians it appeared that when ladies – and more particularly, young unmarried ladies – were of the company, this rule had to be amended. In such company there was a point at which truth had to be concealed beneath an opaque petticoat.

Now the character of the Misses Stephen was such that, from the first, it was taken for granted that the freedoms of Cambridge should be continued in London and that conversational petticoats should be discarded.

'We did not hesitate,' says Vanessa Bell in her memoir, 'to talk of anything,' and she adds:

> 'This was literally true. You could say what you liked about art, sex, or religion; you could also talk freely and very likely dully about the ordinary doings of daily life. There was very little self-consciousness I think in these early gatherings . . . but life was exciting, terrible and amusing and one had to explore it thankful that one could do so freely.'

Such conversations could hardly escape notice, and, having been noticed, could hardly fail to be censured. She continues:

> 'It seemed as if, as soon as our very innocent society got under way and began to have some life in it, hostility was aroused. Perhaps this always happens. Any kind of clique is sneered at by those outside it as a matter of course, and no doubt our ways of behaviour in our own surroundings were sufficiently odd, according to the custom of the day, to stir criticism. Certainly I remember being questioned curiously by a group of young and older people at an ordinary conventional party as to whether we really sat up late talking to young men till all hours of the night. What did we talk about? Who were these young men? etc. They laughed. Even then there was a trace of disapproval.'

No doubt it was in certain respects an innocent society, although even in 1905 a group which contained Lytton Strachey and Clive Bell cannot have been conversationally chaste. It is my impression that Bloomsbury was never promiscuous either in its normal or its homosexual relationships. By modern standards it was restrained in its language and romantic in its attachments. Carnal adventures were justified only by passion, although passion was licence enough; Bloomsbury, while denying that there was such a thing as an impure act, would certainly have recognised and condemned impure states of mind.

There was, both in speech and action, a rapid development between the years 1904 and 1914. I have before me as I write a letter written by a young married woman in 1913, thanking a young man for a charming weekend in the country. She asks whether, after she had left them, her host had spent a pleasant afternoon making love to the two young men who were with him; she draws a vivid though frivolous picture of what may have occurred between them, sparing no details; and ends by recalling that she has left her macintosh in the hall, and asking whether one of the catamites could bring it with him to London?

There is a certain air of conscious bravado about this letter and it was not, so far as I can ascertain, typical of Bloomsbury's epistolatory manners at the period. Nevertheless it shows how rapidly and how far the Victorian age had been left behind.

In his essay on Bloomsbury Clive Bell says of his contemporaries that 'they shared a taste for discussion in pursuit of truth and a contempt for conventional ways of thinking and feeling, contempt for conventional morals if you will.' And he adds: 'Does it not strike you that as much could be said of many collections of young or youngish people in many ages and in many lands? For my part, I find nothing distinctive here.'

Personally I doubt whether any group had ever been so radical in its rejection of sexual taboos. I am not sure. But I am sure that there had never before been a moral adventure of this kind in which women were on a completely equal footing with men.

In this sense Bloomsbury was feminist. It was also more or less feminist in a wider and more usual sense; but whereas nineteenth-century feminism was puritanical and hoped to see male licence curbed by the natural guardians of the home, the feminism of Bloomsbury was libertarian and, while challenging the ethics of a society which saw in the man the natural fount of power and authority, challenged also the entire system of morality on which that power was based. For members of the group the sanctity of the home had no justification save in mutual affection.

Certainly they were not alone in protesting against the irrationality and cruelty of sexual superstition, but I think that they were more persistent and more thoroughgoing than most, if not all, of their contemporaries in their rejection of the claims of authority to establish ethical canons for men and women.

To this theoretical extremism they added a kind of cheerful shamelessness which could shock even those who, in principle, agreed with them. The following incident may serve to illustrate my point. In 1912, when the Post-Impressionist Exhibition closed, there was a ball to celebrate the event. The ladies of Bloomsbury, and their younger friends at the Slade, chose to honour the occasion by disguising themselves as Tahitians (Gauguin had of course been one of the revelations of the exhibitions). Tahitian costume was interpreted as a kind of sarong. Unfortunately the only graphic evidence that I have gives little notion of the nudity of these garments. But in the year 1911, when skirts swept the floor, it was startling. Several respectable ladies hoisted signals of protest and sailed out of the room, and even Roger Fry, although he did not withdraw, entered a mild protest.

I have said enough, I hope, to suggest that, in a society which was almost unbelievably stuffy, Bloomsbury was asking for trouble. Society hardly knew what it would undoubtedly have called 'the worst'; but it knew enough to perceive that this was an atheistical, mocking, libertarian group. Henry James discovered to his distress that the children of his old friend Leslie Stephen were deplorably but unquestionably lacking in those mundane graces in which he himself so exquisitely rejoiced. The liberation of the young meant, inevitably, the distress and sometimes the estrangement of the old. For the Stephen girls in particular, the formation of Bloomsbury was an escape from another world. A determined attempt had been made to bring them out, to launch them into good society where two beautiful young women might fairly hope to encounter eligible young men. The thing was not very well managed, and even if it had been one may doubt whether it would have succeeded. After some efforts it was abandoned and, as Vanessa Bell said in a memoir destined for (but not I think actually read to) the survivors of Old Bloomsbury: 'That was the end of my career in the upper world. I rapidly sank to the lower and have remained there, if I may say so without disrespect to the present company.'

But a price had been paid in boredom and frustration amongst people none of whom, to quote again, 'could have been in this room without making you feel shabby and dirty, so neat and tidy and expensive were their clothes, so utterly unaware that there was any such thing as painting in the world.' The goad of tedium engendered a certain fierceness in its victims. When Vanessa and Virginia escaped to Bloomsbury they were ruthless enough in their measures to lead one pair of respectable philistines to use the ultimate social weapon, the 'cut direct'. Vanessa Bell once described the occasion, the oddity of seeing someone whom she knew very well look right through her, and then the sense of joy and relief as she understood that the break was complete and irrevocable.

In her and, I think, in some other members of the group, the tension that resulted from these and later nonconformities engendered a certain genial brutality which could verge on arrogance. There were many eminently victorian friends whom they never wished to see again; and although, as their ideals began to spread amongst the young, their circle expanded, in some measure they remained a self-enclosed society.

In the development of Bloomsbury up to the year 1914 there are four key dates: 1899, 1904, 1906 and 1910.

As we have seen, Bloomsbury began in Cambridge in 1899. After the death of Sir Leslie Stephen in 1904, the Cambridge element united with a London element. In 1906 Thoby Stephen died and Vanessa Stephen became engaged to Clive Bell; in 1910 the First Post-Impressionist Exhibition was held at the Grafton Galleries.

The death of Thoby Stephen had an effect upon Bloomsbury which it is impossible to calculate; he was an energetic, extrovert

20 Virginia and Leonard Woolf, 1912

21 (*above left*) Duncan Grant, Roger Fry and Vanessa Bell painting Lytton Strachey, just visible behind Roger Fry's canvas, at Asheham in 1913

22 (*above*) Lytton Strachey, still sitting, and Julian Bell

23 (*left*) Duncan Grant's painting of Lytton Strachey

24 Asheham, the Sussex home rented by Virginia Woolf from 1912–19 and much frequented by Bloomsbury friends

25 Clive Bell and Oliver Strachey playing badminton at Asheham in 1913

26 & 27 Studland 1910: (*above*) Clive Bell, Desmond McCarthy, Marjorie Strachey (with manifesto) and Molly McCarthy: (*left*) Virginia Stephen and Clive Bell

character and, if he had lived, would probably have been one of those members of the group who took an active part in politics. The marriage of Clive and Vanessa Bell gave the group two centres instead of one, for the Bells settled at 46 Gordon Square, while Virginia and Adrian Stephen moved to Fitzroy Square. It was there that their neighbour Duncan Grant first met the two younger Stephens and joined in those Thursday conversations of which he has given a lively account in *Horizon*.

Nothing is more indicative of the character of a group than its talk, nothing is more difficult to reconstruct. Even of those later conversations in which I was privileged to join, little now remains. But judging from those and from report, I should say that the talk was not brilliant. By that I mean that there was not much in the way of pyrotechnics, none of that launching of *mots*, that conscious soaring scintillation which one associates with the 'nineties and of which one heard an echo in the conversation of Walter Sickert. It is true that Maynard Keynes was fond of paradox, that Lytton Strachey could suddenly produce remarks of devastating acuteness, and that the whole of Desmond MacCarthy's astonishing charm seemed to lie in his tongue, while Virginia Woolf was able, in later life, to enchant her friends with a peculiar kind of conversational fantasy. But the tone was, I think, derived from G. E. Moore, which meant that there was a certain high seriousness in the conversation despite its gaiety, that there was quite as much argument as gossip, and that in argument it was supposed, at all events, that the contributors were looking for truth, not victory. It meant also that there was a respect for silence, and it says much for the character of the group that although Clive Bell and Roger Fry, together with those whom I have already mentioned, were talkative enough, Saxon Sydney Turner, who had a positive genius for saying nothing, played an important part, while in later years the painters, although they tended to say very little, were an essential element in the company. Bloomsbury at its best might be described in Virginia Woolf's words as producing 'not that hard little electric light that we call brilliance as it pops in and out upon our lips, but the more profound, subtle and subterranean glow which is the rich yellow flame of rational intercourse.'

If we omit E. M. Forster and Roger Fry it is true to say that up to the year 1910 Bloomsbury had produced very little apart from conversation, very little, that is, that could be shown to the world. Lytton Strachey was writing for *The Spectator*, Virginia Stephen for *The Times Literary Supplement*, Maynard Keynes and Saxon Sydney Turner were at the Treasury, neither Clive Bell nor Desmond MacCarthy had published anything serious, Leonard Woolf was still in the jungles of Ceylon.

'I have the impression' writes Duncan Grant, 'that no one had much encouragement for anything they produced. Nor was it looked for. Nothing was expected save complete frankness (of criticism) and a mutual respect for the point of view of each. To work for immediate success never entered anyone's head, perhaps partly because it seemed out of the question. Virginia Stephen was working on her first novel, *The Voyage Out*. It took seven years to finish. But I do not remember that this was thought to be an out of the way length of time in which to produce a novel.'

In 1910, however, immediate success, or at least immediate notoriety, descended upon them. Roger Fry, already a celebrated figure in the world of art and sometime director of the Metropolitan Museum, had become wildly enthusiastic about Cézanne and the younger French painters. He took the Grafton Gallery and gave London its first real taste of the Post-Impressionists. The effect was an explosion of public wrath which, although it has often been described, is barely credible today, and one which made Fry the best-hated man in the London art world.

There was a section of Bloomsbury which could hardly have avoided being drawn into this turmoil. Clive Bell as a critic, Vanessa Bell and Duncan Grant as painters, were completely whole-hearted in their acceptance of Roger Fry's views – if not of all his theories – but for the rest the business must have been puzzling. Cambridge had never discussed art and Lytton Strachey, although he purchased modern paintings – as did Maynard Keynes and Saxon Sydney Turner – was not at all sure, to begin with at all events, that he liked them. But it was hard, when Roger Fry had a cause at heart, for his friends not to find themselves involved in it. Desmond MacCarthy was made

Cover for the catalogue of the Second Post-Impressionist Exhibition, 1912

Vision Volumes and Recession, Homage to Roger Fry by Walter Richard Sickert, c. 1911

Secretary of the first exhibition and Leonard Woolf, on his return from Ceylon, acted for a time as Secretary to the second show. His account of the matter is illuminating:

> 'The first room was filled with Cézanne water-colours. The highlights in the second room were two enormous pictures of more than life-size figures by Matisse and three or four Picassos. There was also a Bonnard, and a good picture by Marchand. Large numbers of people came to the exhibition, and nine out of ten of them either roared with laughter at the pictures or were enraged by them . . . The whole business gave me a lamentable view of human nature, its rank stupidity and uncharitableness . . . Hardly any of them made the slightest attempt to look at, let alone understand, the pictures, and the same inane questions or remarks were repeated to me all day long. And every now and then some well-groomed, red-faced gentleman, oozing the undercut of the best beef and the most succulent of chops, carrying his top hat and grey suede gloves, would come up to my table and abuse the pictures and me with the greatest rudeness.'

Roger Fry, although he was considerably older than his friends and although his intellectual background was different – he had never been a disciple of Moore – became very much a member of Bloomsbury. It was through him, rather than through Clive Bell, that the group established a close *rapport* with Paris, the Paris of Matisse, Derain, Picasso, Segonzac, Apollinaire and Vildrac. It was through his influence, warmly seconded by Clive Bell, Duncan Grant and Vanessa Bell, and to a lesser extent by Lytton Strachey, that Bloomsbury became, on the whole, francophile. It was certainly in part under his influence that Clive Bell wrote *Art* (1914).

Roger Fry was so closely linked by friendship with the other members of Bloomsbury that they could hardly be expected to remain indifferent, whatever their own aesthetic views, to the popular clamour that he had aroused. It raised, in a new way, the issue of tolerance. In an essay entitled '*Avons nous changé tout cela?*' (1913), Lytton Strachey accused Professor Bury of being too optimistic in believing that the world had at last learnt to be

Letterhead for the Omega Workshops, designed by Wyndham Lewis, 1913

tolerant; all we had done, he declared, was to effect a 'transition from the metaphysical to the ethical species of persecution, and from this perhaps we might pass to aesthetic intolerance . . . After the late fulminations of Sir William Richmond against Post-Impressionism, nobody could be very much surprised if a stake were set up tomorrow for Mr Roger Fry in the courtyard of Burlington House.' For Bloomsbury this was a first taste of public execration and it was, though comic, unpleasant. On the other hand, for those who were deeply committed to the Post-Impressionist movement – and of course this included a great many people who had nothing to do with Bloomsbury – the years between 1910 and 1914 were in the highest degree exhilarating.

In 1912 Roger Fry invited Duncan Grant to lunch at Durbins, his home near Guildford, to meet some dealers who, Fry hoped, might be of use to the young painter. Grant failed to turn up; he had not enough money to pay the fare, or rather he had saved enough for the excursion but then put the money in a safe place and lost it. The incident was important. Fry decided that something must be done for young and penniless artists. If they could not sell pictures then they might decorate chairs, and how splendid it would be if Post-Impressionism, a style capable of decorative application, could sweep through the furniture shops of London. A market existed; led by that fabulous creature – for once the word fabulous seems justifiable, since she has been the heroine of so many fables – that fantastic, baroque flamingo, Lady Ottoline Morrell, an element in society was beginning to look with curiosity and a little favour on the aesthetic innovations of the time. The times seemed propitious, and Fry founded the Omega Workshops.

The Omega came into existence in July 1913 and was, almost immediately, shaken by the most appalling internal schism.

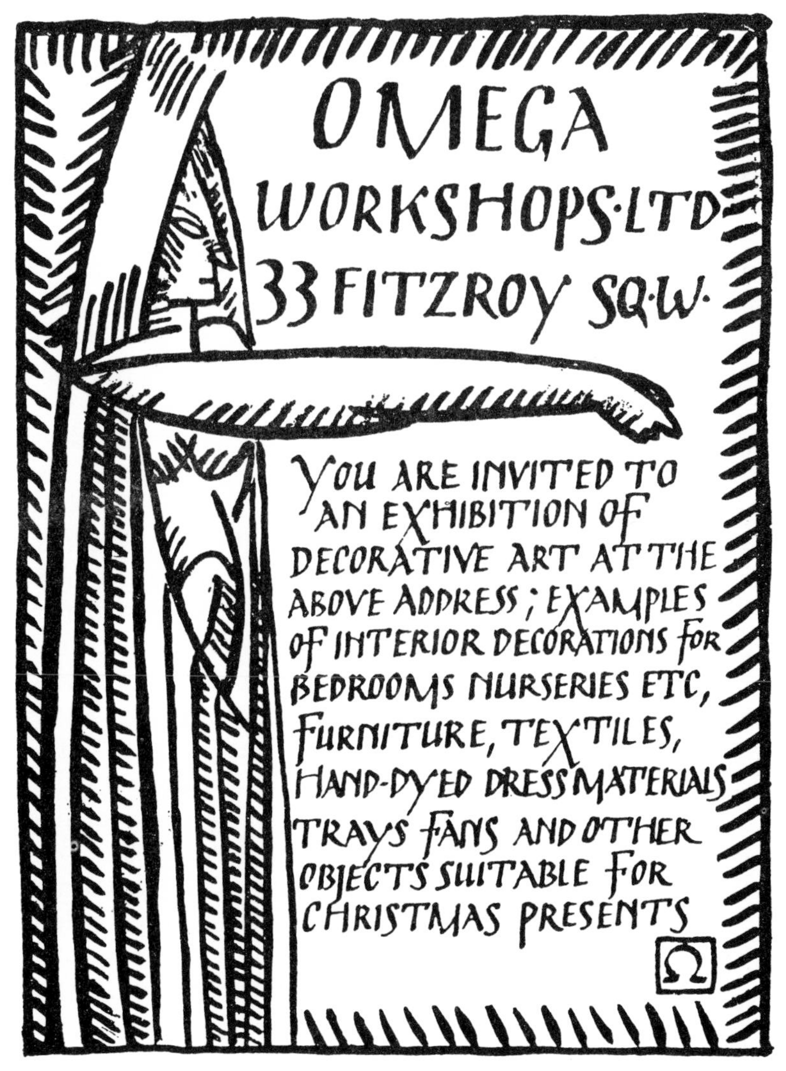

Advertisement for an exhibition at the Omega Workshops, 1913

Together with another student of this period I have already attempted to give a full account of this matter, but here I would like to recite the main facts of the case.[7]

Wyndham Lewis, with three of his friends, became dissatisfied with Fry's management of the business. They came across evidence which seemed to show that Fry had acted in a dishonourable manner, and responded by circulating a letter in which Fry was accused of chicanery, dishonesty and double-dealing. This was sent to the friends, customers and shareholders of the Omega Workshops. The blow was a heavy one. Aimed at Fry and at the Omega, it could discredit the one and destroy the other, and it was in the highest degree actionable.

To Fry and his friends, who did not know all the circumstances of the case, it must have seemed an act of pure malevolence. They had in their hands a document that would have made Fry's innocence apparent and, as they must have thought, would confound and humiliate his accuser. Naturally they considered the possibility of bringing an action or at least of making a public statement. In the end they did nothing; there was no lawsuit and no reply.

Now this refusal to meet violence with counter-violence, which was, I think, endorsed by all those members of the group who were in any way concerned with the business, was pacific but not charitable. Fry and his friends realised that Lewis was spoiling for a fight, and saw that a refusal to meet him on his own grounds was, even though they would be the victors, far from kind. They could not know that Lewis really did believe himself to be in the right, and thus they failed to grasp how intensely he suffered from being dismissed without a blow. It is hardly astonishing that, for the rest of his life, Lewis believed that he was being persecuted by Bloomsbury and, above all, by Roger Fry; it is after all more comfortable to suppose that one is being persecuted than to believe that one is disregarded, and this anguished sense of injustice finds its echo in the violent fantasies of Lewis's friend and recorder, Sir John Rothenstein.

The entire incident gives an illuminating view of the way in which Bloomsbury could react to provocation, with a pacifism which was not merely uncharitable but positively insulting. There was a certain wounding contempt in the refusal to return blow

28 Ham Spray House, from 1924 the home of Lytton Strachey

29 Francis Birrell, Lytton Strachey and Saxon Sydney Turner at Ham Spray House

30 Durbins, near Guildford, the house that Roger Fry built for himself in 1909

31/2/3 At Durbins: (*above left*) Clive Bell, (*above right*) Molly McCarthy and (*left*) Vanessa Bell

34 Charleston; from 1916 the Sussex home of Clive and Vanessa Bell and Duncan Grant

35 Vanessa Bell in the garden at Charleston wearing a costume designed by her and Duncan Grant for Mélisande in Copeau's production of *Pelléas et Mélisande*

36 At Monks House, the Woolfs' Sussex home: Maynard Keynes (*extréme left*), E. M. Forster, Lydia Keynes (Lopokova) and Roger Fry

37 On the terrace at Charleston: Roger Fry, Desmond McCarthy and Clive Bell, 1933

38 At Charleston: Duncan Grant and E. M. Forster (*standing*), Clive Bell and Mary Hutchinson

39 (*left to right*) Frances Marshall (later Partridge), Quentin Bell, Julian Bell, Duncan Grant, Clive Bell, Beatrice Mayor; (*seated*) Roger Fry and Raymond Mortimer in the foreground

40 The library at Ham Spray House

41 Maynard and Lydia Keynes at 46 Gordon Square

for blow, a certain air of conscious superiority, the superiority of one who disdains to fight. There was also something else: in discussing the matter fifty years later I found that those who remembered the incident could recall only the pain of separation from the friends of Wyndham Lewis whom they liked. The *casus belli*, and the documents that would prove Fry's innocence, had long been forgotten; they took it for granted that Lewis had been silly and that his inventions could be dismissed as being unworthy of discussion. All this was unimportant; a broken friendship was a much graver and sadder matter. They judged the question of who was in the right on grounds of character and on these grounds very properly exonerated Fry without question, while doing rather less than justice to Wyndham Lewis; but what remained at the end was not a question of justice or injustice but of friends hurt and friendships broken. It was very much in these terms that they were to consider the larger conflict that was soon to follow.

3

The War

Bloomsbury, as we have seen, was very largely a product of Cambridge. When one comes to that crucial period in its development which starts in August 1914 it is perhaps relevant to ask how Cambridge reacted to the war. Lowes Dickinson, a friend of most of the Bloomsbury figures and, in particular, of Roger Fry, has left an account from which I quote:

> 'To me the worse kind of disillusionment was that connected with universities and historians. Hardly a voice was raised from those places and persons to maintain the light of truth. Like the rest, moved by passion, by fear, by the need to be in the swim, those who should have been the leaders followed the crowd down a steep place . . . I learned once for all that students, those whose business it would seem to be to keep the light of truth burning in a storm, are like other men, blindly patriotic, savagely vigilant, cowardly and false when public opinion once begins to run strong. The younger dons and even the older ones disappeared into war work. All discussion, all pursuit of truth ceased as in a moment. To win the war or to hide safely among the winners became the only preoccupation. Abroad was heard only the sound of the guns, at home only the ceaseless patter of a propaganda utterly indifferent to truth.'[8]

Cambridge, in fact, like the vast majority of the nation, had been converted to the religion of nationalism; it was a powerful, a terrible, at times a very beautiful magic. The communal emotions of love and hatred found expression in astonishing acts of gallantry, credulity and folly. The British people, like all the other peoples of Europe, was ready to defy the foe in circumstances which called for unexampled heroism and fortitude. Equally it was ready to believe in the absolute goodness of our cause, the absolute badness of the enemy and all his works. To this end the family name of the monarch was to be changed by deed poll and kindergartens were henceforward to be known as infant schools; German art was to be expelled from our galleries and German music from our concert halls. These, it might appear, were measures which could bring no substantial advantage to the allied powers, but then the same could be said of the greater part of their military operations. The purpose was not practical, it was religious.

Today these extravagances seem odd, while the continued belief in imminent victory, in the genius of our military leaders, in the invariable heroism of our troops and the sterling sincerity of our politicians, seems pathetic enough when set against the hideous blunders, the senseless carnage, the political chicanery and the vastly profitable trade for which they formed a screen. To us, as to Lowes Dickinson, it is shocking that the intellectuals should so easily have embraced a system of belief in which there was no place for the intellectual virtues. But for them this faith was particularly attractive. The intellectual tends to be socially isolated, to be conscious of his own personality, to be over-civilised. War offers him an escape into the community, an escape from his own personal problems, a release from social bonds and the opportunity for a return to nature, that state of nature in which the simpler kinds of social affection, the primitive motives of aggression and self-immolation are sanctioned and encouraged.

Intellectually this country was ill-prepared for war; both the pacifists and their adversaries were taken by surprise. There was indeed what one may call a war party, a party which, influenced no doubt by the Catholic writers of France, preached violence and anti-semitism; but the very extravagance of writers such as Chesterton and Saki suggests a lack of seriousness – they were prepared rather for a pillow fight than for a European conflict. When the war did come their gestures were in some ways inadequate, but at least their position was clear. Much less clear was the position of writers like Wells and G. M. Trevelyan who had, in one way or another, been liberal and pacifist but who now found themselves converted to the religion of Nationalism.

The position of Bloomsbury at this crisis was also not entirely clear, that is to say that it was not uniform: there were some who were conscientious objectors and others who were ready to fight or to serve the government in various ways. But they none of them, so to speak, 'believed in' the war, and they refused, resolutely, to be religious about it.

Now, to the convert, no one, not even the enemy, is as odious as the stubborn unbeliever. Take the case of H. G. Wells – a very complete convert to the religion of war. He was irritated by what seemed to him the absurd fuss that was made about the sufferings of the conscientious objectors. He described the pacifists of Garsington and the 1917 Club, of which Bloomsbury formed an important element, as the 'genteel Whigs'. The genteel Whig was

> 'a little, loose, shy, independent person . . . He is acutely aware of possessing an exceptionally fine intelligence, but he is entirely unconscious of a fundamental unreality . . . It was of course natural and inevitable that the German onslaught upon Belgium and civilisation generally should strike these recluse minds not as a monstrous ugly wickedness to be resisted and overcome at any cost, but merely as a nerve-racking experience. Guns were going off on both sides. The Genteel Whig was chiefly conscious of a repulsive vast excitement all about him in which many people did inelegant and irrational things. They waved flags – nasty little flags. This child of all the ages, this last fruit of the gigantic and tragic tree of life, could do no more than stick its fingers in its ears and say, "Oh, please do *all* stop!" And then as the strain grew intenser and intenser set itself with feeble pawings now to clamber "*Au-dessus de la Mêlée*", and now to – in some weak way – stop the conflict. ("*Au-dessus de la Mêlée*," as the man said when the bull gored his sister.)'[9]

Wells's final thrust is an echo of the question frequently put to conscientious objectors: 'What would you do if a German officer tried to rape your sister?' Lytton Strachey's celebrated reply: 'I should try to get between them,' represents precisely the attitude – an attitude at once intelligent and irreverent – to which Wells objected. The war was an affair of honour, not of reason. Reasoning is out of place when your sister's virtue is in danger; in that situation you must follow your intuitions. Wells's analysis of the attitude of pacifists such as Strachey and Clive Bell and Duncan Grant was not unintelligent; they did indeed regard the war as horrible, unnecessary and fundamentally ridiculous – a war about nothing, a war that could do no good to anyone. Talk of honour, courage and patriotism was no more to be regarded than the taunts that one child flings at another daring it to risk a dash across a busy street.

I doubt whether anybody in Bloomsbury was very much hurt by H. G. Wells's strictures; the quarrel with Rupert Brooke was another matter. He had been a close friend, and the estrangement was certainly very distressing to Virginia Woolf, who liked him very much. In fact, however, his attitude to the war was only the final stage in a quarrel between Brooke and Bloomsbury. He had already denounced the 'subtle degradation of the collective atmosphere of the people in these regions – people I find pleasant and remarkable as individuals,' nor is this surprising when we consider that Brooke had already turned from a rational to an intuitive view of life. He wrote:

> 'And I also think, now, that this passion for goodness and loathing of evil is the most valuable and important thing in us. And that it must not in any way be stifled nor compelled to wait upon exact judgment . . . If ever in life one detects evil one should count five, perhaps, but then hit out . . . it's the only battle that counts.'

How then did one know evil? One knew it by intuition, like the Samoans who 'are not so foolish as to think [but whose] intelligence is incredibly lively and subtle.' Brooke's intuitions told him that the world is only to be saved by virility. 'This mixing of the sexes is all wrong, male is male and female is female . . . manliness in man is the one hope of the world.' Rupert Brooke had drawn his sword long before the war started; now he wanted to use it.[10]

> Leave the sick hearts that honour could not move,
> And half men, and their dirty songs and dreary,
> And all the little emptiness of love.

Rupert Brooke had suffered from a nervous breakdown in 1911 and he was afflicted by an almost insane belief that Lytton Strachey had wrecked his private life. No doubt his attitude to Bloomsbury was in a large measure the result of personal rather than theoretical antipathies. Nevertheless his belief in the value of intuition was, as Christopher Hassall has pointed out, very close to that of D. H. Lawrence. He too might have said: 'My great religion is the belief in the blood, the flesh, as being wiser than the intellect.' Lawrence, who clearly hated the war, was unable sometimes to resist the great communal emotions of those years so that he could exclaim, almost against his own will: '. . . I am mad with rage myself. I would like to kill a million Germans – two millions . . .'

The relationship of Lawrence to Bloomsbury must be considered in some detail, for it has been the subject of extraordinary confusion.

It was a tenuous, brief and, so far as it went, a painful connection. Lawrence did not know, or barely knew, Clive and Vanessa Bell, Roger Fry, Lytton Strachey, Desmond and Molly MacCarthy, Leonard and Virginia Woolf, Gerald Shove, Adrian Stephen and H. T. J. Norton. I think he may have known Sydney Waterlow. In his letters he mentions the work of some of them and mentions it with distaste. Clive Bell he thought a fool, Roger Fry a bad painter, Leonard Woolf wrote sentences which 'take a bit of reading'; he believed that Desmond MacCarthy had treated him badly. But he seems to have had no very deep feelings about any of these characters and he does not discuss Bloomsbury collectively, although Frieda Lawrence may be voicing his opinions when she says that 'There was no flow of the milk of human kindness in that group of Lytton Strachey and Bloomsburies, not even a trickle. They were too busy being witty and clever.'

Lawrence did however feel the strongest aversion for two people who were unquestionably 'Bloomsbury', Duncan Grant and Maynard Keynes, and for one person who belongs doubtfully to the group, Francis Birrell. He also knew Morgan Forster.

Of the uneasy friendship with Forster little need be said. It was based upon mutual admiration and mutual exasperation; it did not last long; it ended in coolness rather than heat. Forster was *not* one of those people who made Lawrence dream of black beetles; it was Keynes and Grant and Birrell who did this, and it seems worth while to ask why this was the case.

The quarrel with them, if so one-sided an affair can be thus described, resulted from three encounters during the year 1915.

In each case an attempt had been made by one of Lawrence's admirers to introduce him to new friends; in each case the attempt ended in disaster.

In January 1915 David Garnett, a fairly old and very devoted friend of Lawrence, brought him and Morgan Forster to Duncan Grant's studio. Lawrence proceeded, with characteristic vigour, to tell Duncan Grant what was wrong with his painting: 'It was not simply that the pictures were bad – hopelessly bad – but they were worthless because Duncan was full of the wrong ideas.' It was a long and remorseless lecture during which the painter made no attempt to defend himself or even to speak.

'This interview,' wrote Duncan Grant, 'was painful to me because I felt that Lawrence was quite unsympathetic to what I was trying to do at the moment.'

It was even more painful for David Garnett for, as he says: 'The blast of Lawrence's attack had been directed at Duncan, who no doubt felt that he had suffered an unexpected assault, but *he* had lost nothing. I knew that the hopes I had nursed of happy hours with them both was vain. My two friends would never understand each other.'

The second encounter took place in Cambridge; here Bertrand Russell effected the introductions. Like most people, Russell had been charmed and impressed by Lawrence, and he believed that he could learn from one whose modes of apprehension were so different from his own; together they discussed a revolution that would cleanse the body politic of its many diseases by means which never became very clear. They would begin by giving lectures together; but first Lawrence was to come to Cambridge.

'Also I feel frightfully important coming to Cambridge – quite momentous the occasion is to me,' wrote Lawrence, adding, rather nervously: 'I don't want to be horribly impressed and intimidated, but I'm afraid I may be.' Whether he was in fact impressed or intimidated we cannot tell, but certainly he was unhappy. The visit was a failure and a meeting with Maynard Keynes was particularly unrewarding.

A month later, in April 1915, David Garnett, still desperately trying to unite his friends, brought Francis Birrell to stay with the Lawrences in Sussex. This was the most disastrous meeting of them all. After it was over Lawrence wrote to Lady Ottoline Morrell:

> 'To hear these young people talking really fills me with black fury: they talk endlessly, but endlessly – and never, never a good or real thing said. Their attitude is so irreverent and so blatant. They are cased, each in a hard little shell of his own, and out of this they talk words. There is never, for one second, any outgoing of feeling, and no reverence, not a crumb or grain of reverence. I cannot stand it. I *will not* have people like this – I had rather be alone. They made me dream in the night of a beetle that bites like a scorpion. But I killed it – a very large beetle. I scotched it and it ran off – but I came upon it again, and killed it. It is this horror of little swarming selves that I can't stand.'

And to David Garnett himself:

> 'Never bring Birrell to see me any more. There is something nasty about him like black beetles. He is horrible and unclean. I feel I should go mad when I think of your set, Duncan Grant and Keynes and Birrell. It makes me dream of beetles. In Cambridge I had a similar dream. I had felt it slightly before in the Stracheys. But it came full upon me in Keynes and in Duncan Grant. And yesterday I knew it again in Birrell – you must leave these friends, these beetles. Birrell and Duncan Grant are done for forever. Keynes I am not sure – when I saw Keynes that morning in Cambridge it was one of the crises of my life. It sent me mad with misery and hostility and rage. The Oliviers and such girls are wrong. I could sit and howl in a corner like a child. I feel so bad about it all.'

Frieda Lawrence enclosed a note written in a kindlier spirit to which Lawrence added a postscript:

'You have always known the wrong people, Harolds and Olivier girls. Love. D. H. Lawrence.'

Obviously these three social mishaps were connected, connected at all events in Lawrence's mind. The offence of the young man who talked too much was related to that of the painter who held his tongue and both with those of the Cambridge economist. David Garnett makes this clear enough in his narrative:

'Lawrence had really forced me to break with him because of his dislike, and perhaps jealousy, of my friends. He hated their respect for reason and contempt for intuition and instinct.'

Maynard Keynes, following the same line of thought, sees the conflict between Lawrence and Garnett's friends as something altogether ideological. In an essay entitled *My Early Beliefs* he uses Lawrence's outbursts as a text on which to hang a lay sermon. Bloomsbury, he had come to believe, had misused the philosophy of G.E. Moore; it had rejected traditional wisdom, it had become immoralist:

> 'And if I imagine us as coming under the observation of Lawrence's ignorant, jealous, irritable, hostile eyes, what a combination of qualities we offered to arouse his passionate distaste; this thin rationalism skipping on the crust of lava, ignoring both the reality and the value of the vulgar passions, joined to libertinism and comprehensive irreverence, too clever by half for such an earthy character as Bunny, seducing with its intellectual chic such a portent as Ottoline, a regular skin-poison. All this was very unfair to poor, silly, well-meaning us. But that is why I say that there must have been just a grain of truth when Lawrence said that we were "done for".'

Dr Leavis, taking Maynard Keynes's argument as he finds it, that is to say seeing the whole thing as a straight confrontation between Lawrence and 'the Cambridge-Bloomsbury milieu' (an entity which he does not define), goes on to say that Lawrence was in no way jealous. He was not 'impressed or intimidated', far from it, he realised that he had encountered an inferior 'civilisation' composed of immature and, by his standards, ill-educated people whom he very properly 'loathed and despised'.

Now I should like to say something about the circumstances in which Maynard Keynes's paper was originally read. It was in the summer of 1938, the summer before Munich; the audience consisted of the Memoir Club, that is to say a more or less Bloomsbury audience, and two persons who were not in any real sense Bloomsbury, Jane Bussy, a niece of Lytton Strachey, and myself. A certain part of the paper was addressed to, or at, us – the younger generation. Maynard knew that we, and indeed some of his contemporaries, considered that he had become very reactionary. His plea for the traditional values, his attacks on Marxism, his sympathy for Lawrence's attitude towards intuition as opposed to reason was meant to shock and irritate us; it succeeding in doing so and I have no doubt that he enjoyed himself enormously, particularly since he must have realised that we (like Dr Leavis) had been hoodwinked. We had failed to notice that the sermon had very little to do with the text.

Keynes and Leavis assume that what offended and disgusted Lawrence was the intellectual quality of Bloomsbury. But Lawrence himself never says this. He never talks about Bloomsbury. He was annoyed by the 'young people', the 'swarming little selves' of his letter to Lady Ottoline Morrell, and of these we may assume that Francis Birrell (who was near-Bloomsbury) was the worst offender. But who were the others? The only other young people, apart from David Garnett himself, were Meynells, Farjeons and Radfords of whom Lawrence was very fond and who certainly did not induce nightmares. It was the Bloomsbury characters who did this and whom he associated with black beetles.

Now it is arguable that it was the 'brittle' conversation of Francis Birrell and Maynard Keynes that produced this nightmare in Lawrence's mind. But what about Duncan Grant?

Duncan Grant is most specifically and pointedly referred to as a prime mover of black beetles and yet it is clear from David Garnett's account that he never produced any opinions, or indeed any conversation of any kind whatsoever.

It is true that he did produce some pictures. Can we then discover in Duncan Grant's work some pictorial equivalent for the arguments of Keynes or the gossip of Birrell? Such an argument, almost impossibly difficult to sustain in any circumstances, becomes untenable when one learns that Lawrence had an embroidery designed by Duncan Grant in his own house at Zennor. This was a year after his root-and-branch denunciation of Grant's work and would seem to argue an almost incomprehensible degree of critical inconsistency unless we may believe that Lawrence was in truth criticising, not the work of art, but the artist himself.[11]

That this was in fact the case, that Lawrence was concerned rather with personalities than with ideas is made probable by the fact that he denounces people who had nothing to do with Bloomsbury: Bryn, Daphne, Noel and Margery Olivier ('the Olivier girls') and Harold Hobson.

Is it not clear that Lawrence is concerned only in a very minor way with the conscious waking world of rival ideologies and much more with the half-world of the dream? For some reason he felt himself menaced by David Garnett's friends; it was not simply that they were wrong about the Universe, they were 'horrible, nasty and unclean'. What then had they in common to make them so detestable?

I have already supplied the answer. They were David Garnett's friends, and more than that they were all, in one way or another, attractive.

Garnett himself was amazed that Lawrence should have misjudged Francis Birrell so completely. 'In retrospect the most astonishing thing was Lawrence's dislike of Frankie. Everyone else who ever knew him, of whatever age or sex or nationality or class, was charmed and delighted by him.'

Those who know him must feel the same astonishment and might indeed use exactly the same words about Duncan Grant. But in fact Lawrence was far too perceptive *not* to feel what so many others have felt: 'We liked Duncan Grant very much. I really liked him . . .' And again, 'When Birrell comes – tired and a bit lost and wondering – I love him.'

But it was this, precisely, that constituted the offence. Keynes, Grant, Birrell, they were all very delightful people. They could also be imagined, when once the demon of jealousy had taken command, as rivals, not rival intellectual influences but sexual rivals. So could the Olivier girls; but they were not so agonisingly dangerous as the men. Lawrence gives a clear indication of his suspicions and of his horror when, speaking of Birrell, he talks of 'men lovers of men, they give me a sense of corruption, almost of putrescence, that I dream of beetles. It is abominable.'

Lawrence's nightmare insects were in fact not intellectual but erotic phenomena:

> 'Yesterday, at Worthing, there were many soldiers. Can I ever tell you how ugly they were. "To insects – sensual lust." I like sensual lust – but insectwise, no – it is obscene. I like men to be beasts – but insects – one insect mounted on another – oh God! The soldiers at Worthing are like that – they remind me of lice or bugs: "to insects sensual lust". They will murder their officers one day. They are teeming insects. What massive creeping hell is let loose nowadays.'

Lawrence's prose is sometimes close to the poetry of delirium. It is suggestive rather than explicit; but here at least no one will suppose that he is talking about the intellectual attitudes of Bloomsbury. And yet, how the images recall those of the letter to Ottoline Morrell – 'it is this horror of little swarming selves I can't stand.'

Is it not possible that Lawrence felt himself menaced, not so much by an external as by an internal force? Could it not be that by discovering, or rather suspecting, homosexual passion, not only in others but within himself, he brought forth swarming creatures from the recesses of his mind that could be scotched but not killed, and may we not read the letter to David Garnett as the angry reproach of a jealous lover tortured, not only by his own imagined fears, but by the emergence of his own, unavowable inner demons? Thus read, the letters make good sense, while as a statement of intellectual principles they appear ludicrous. I offer this as a possible explanation – no more. But I am convinced that Lawrence's nightmares had much more to do with his own psyche than with any deficiencies, real or imaginary, in the intellectual outlook of Bloomsbury.

I have dwelt upon this passage in the life of D. H. Lawrence partly because it seems to me interesting in itself, partly because it provides another example of the way in which scholars can be misled when they talk about Bloomsbury. Consider the fate of

Dr Leavis. Misled by Maynard Keynes, he discusses Lawrence's repugnance for the 'Cambridge-Bloomsbury milieu' and appears seriously to believe that this is what Lawrence would have found at Cambridge in 1915. He attacks Keynes when that author is dealing with the beliefs of young men at King's and Trinity around 1904 by quoting Lawrence's remarks about a completely different set of people whom he met ten years later.[12]

It must be allowed that this kind of muddled thinking is made easy by the fact that Lawrence's ideology was almost completely opposed to anything that can be described as a 'Bloomsbury ideology'. But, during the war, the intellectual battle against Lawrence was fought not by Bloomsbury or by anyone in Bloomsbury but by Bertrand Russell. In his account of the matter Russell concludes that 'Lawrence had developed the whole philosophy of fascism before the politicians had thought of it.' This is, at the very least, an over-simplification. Lawrence was not in any real sense a nationalist or a racialist. His day-dream politics were too idiosyncratic to form the basis of anyone's political thinking; they resemble both in their character and their complete divorce from real life the political fantasies of Ruskin. It is true that Lawrence believed in an authoritarian régime, that he had a fervent belief in blood consciousness and insisted upon the virtues of obedience. All this was very properly rejected by Russell and would have been rejected by any one of the people whom I have described as 'Bloomsbury'. But fortunately it would have been rejected by a great many other people, and in saying that Bloomsbury was opposed to Lawrence's political ideas we do not come very close to a useful definition.

It is more useful to look at Lawrence's charge that 'in these young people' there was 'never, for one second, any outgoing . . . of reverence, not a crumb or grain of reverence.' In 1915 Bloomsbury could hardly be described as a group of young people, but it could be described as irreverent. Leonard Woolf accepts the charge in a passage which may be quoted:

> 'If "to revere" means, as the dictionary says, "to regard as sacred or exalted, to hold in religious respect", then we did not revere, we had no reverence for anything or anyone, and so far

> as I am concerned, I think we were completely right . . . The dictionary, however, gives an alternative meaning for the word "revere"; it may mean to "to regard with deep respect and warm approbation". It is not true that we lacked reverence for everything and everyone in that sense of the word. After questioning the truth and utility of everything and after refusing to swallow anything or anyone on the mere "authority" of anyone, in fact after exercising our own judgment, there were many things and persons regarded by us with "deep respect and warm approbation": truth, beauty, works of art, some customs, friendships, love, many living men and women and many of the dead.'[13]

This however was a form of reverence of which D. H. Lawrence would hardly have approved, for in it scepticism was never abandoned and the reverential attitude was subject always to reason.

Now irreverence is the great weapon of minorities; it is an engine for teasing the powerful. Bloomsbury was always in some degree at war with the Establishment, and from an early date made it clear that nothing, or at all events very little, was to be sacred.

'It had seemed to me ever since I was very young . . . that anyone who took up an attitude of authority over anyone else was necessarily also someone who offered a leg to pull.'

The quotation is from Adrian Stephen's account of how, in 1910, he and a party of friends, including his sister Virginia and Duncan Grant, hoodwinked the British Navy and were shown the secrets of its latest vessel, the *Dreadnought*, by pretending to be the Emperor of Abyssinia and his suite. Adrian Stephen and the ringleader, Horace Cole, had previously considered the possibility of disguising themselves as German officers and taking a platoon across the frontier of Alsace-Lorraine: such was the incredible insouciance of that epoch.

'. . . If everyone shared my feelings towards the great armed forces of the world, the world (might) be a happier place to live in. However I don't pretend that I had a moral to preach. I only felt that armies and suchlike bodies presented legs that were almost irresistible.'[14]

'The Novel' from *Twelve Original Woodcuts* by Roger Fry, 1921

The agonised and outraged reactions on the part of Adrian Stephen's relations, some of whom were naval officers, arose from the feeling expressed by one of them that 'His Majesty's ships are not suitable objects for practical jokes.' A similar hoax played upon the Mayor of Cambridge was felt by the same people to be excusable and indeed funny, for the Mayor of Cambridge was a grocer, whereas to hoax an officer and a gentleman was a sin against the gods of Empire, an outrage, an irreverence.

Roger Fry evoked a similar reaction when, reviewing a posthumous exhibition of the works of Alma Tadema, he declared that the painter had 'undoubtedly conveyed the information that the people of that interesting and remote period' (the Roman Empire) 'had their furniture, clothes, even their splendid marble villas made of highly scented soap.'

This, in what was in a sense an obituary, was felt to be unpardonable. 'Mr Fry,' said Sir William Richmond, 'must not be surprised if he is boycotted by decent society.'[15]

To these examples of Bloomsbury irreverence I would add one more that shows the spirit of scepticism, that 'questioning of the truth and utility of everything' to which Leonard Woolf refers. 'I could be wrong,' said Roger Fry, 'about Cézanne.' It is true that he added, 'but I really don't think that I am,' but the remark conveys a little of the resolute determination to take nothing on trust which made Bloomsbury sceptical, even where it felt deeply, and ribald when faced by the great public deities.

The war made Bloomsbury's scepticism a matter almost of principle, and its most characteristic reaction to the conflict was an essay in irreverence. It was not the only reaction; several of the members faced tribunals, Clive Bell made a serious and outright attack upon the war in his pamphlet entitled *Peace at Once*, while Leonard Woolf, having been rejected by a medical board, devoted himself to the study of International Government in the hope of achieving some kind of decent settlement when the conflict ended.

But Bloomsbury's most characteristic offering was *Eminent Victorians*, which was published in 1918. It made its author famous at once. A number of people disliked it very much; but nobody doubted that it was a brilliant performance and a large public found it enormously enjoyable.

I believe that one reason for its colossal success was the discovery that our household Gods were human after all. It was time – exactly the right time – to cut them down to size. After all were they not ultimately responsible for the catastrophe? Lytton Strachey wrote:

> 'The Victorian Age, great in so many directions, was not great in criticism, in humour, in the realistic apprehension of life. It was an age of self-complacency and self-contradiction. Even its atheists (Lord Morley was one of them) were religious. The religious atmosphere fills his book, and blurs every outline. We are shown Mr Gladstone through a haze of reverence, and Emerson, and Marcus Aurelius. We begin to long for a little of the cynicism and scepticism of, precisely, the Age of Diderot, Rousseau, and Voltaire. Perhaps – who knows? – if Lord Morley and his contemporaries had been less completely devoid of those unamiable and unedifying qualities, the history of the world would have been more fortunate. The heartless,

irreverent, indecent eighteenth century produced the French Revolution. The Age of Victoria produced – what?'

A reverential attitude might protect not only the secular artifice of religion but the magic of the Imperial idea, the poetical glories of war as celebrated by Lord Tennyson and that kind of genteel philistinism which is bred in prefects' studies and playing-fields. The Lives of Manning, Gordon, Florence Nightingale and Thomas Arnold might serve to exhibit these idols in an unflattering light. Under the circumstances *Eminent Victorians* was, almost, a tract for the times.

But obviously Strachey's *Eminent Victorians* are not mere pegs to serve an argument; they appear, not as heroes nor as villains, but as human beings – it is this that makes their biographies so readable, and in truth Strachey himself is not attacking, or is only half attacking, the age in which they lived. It might have been disastrous but it was fascinating and, when he came to consider the Queen herself, the portrait that he paints is not disagreeable. He accepts the aesthetic temper of his time, disliking Victorian art and believing that 'artists will never be fair to the Victorian Age . . . But if men of science and men of action were not inarticulate we should hear a different story.' What he objects to in fact is the irrational side of the nineteenth century. What he admired was its scepticism.

In 1918, however, Strachey was hailed or condemned as an iconoclast, justly so in that his method of considering history, whether it was the history of the nineteenth, the eighteenth or the sixteenth century, was essentially irreverent. Where Froude and Macaulay, Carlyle and G. M. Trevelyan, approach history ideologically and discover a hero in whom to embody their ideology, drawing Henry VIII and William III, Cromwell and Garibaldi a little larger than life, Strachey is consistently unheroic and can see the mean, the ridiculous side even, of those characters with whom he is most in sympathy.

By 1918 heroism was at a discount. Before the war it had been a rarity, a scarce and highly valued commodity; then it was brought within the reach of thousands, first inflated and then devalued. Moreover, people had begun to see that, in this war at any rate, heroism was a rather anonymous business. The leaders, the statesmen and generals seemed to be entrepreneurs rather than actual producers of heroism. A certain scepticism, a certain uneasiness, replaced the glorious certainties of 1914. The war poets began to speak in a new tone of voice. In a word the mood was one of disenchantment, and in that mood the British public was ready to listen to what Bloomsbury had to say.

4

Bloomsbury after 1918

'I fancy sometimes the world changes. I think I see reason spreading.' Virginia Woolf wrote those words in 1928. They now appear absurdly optimistic and yet, for a time during the nineteen-twenties, it seemed possible that she might not be mistaken.

The period between 1924 and 1931 may be likened to a short winter's day before the long night of fascism, but it was sufficient to allow Bloomsbury a moment of efflorescence, a time in which to make its mark and, in so doing, to lose its identity. When the last horrors of war, civil war and famine were over, when the cost had been counted, and the dead, when the allies had quarrelled with each other and discovered that they had created nothing more permanent than the Russian Revolution, it was not hard to see that there was, after all, something to be said for Bloomsbury's disbelief in the war. In other directions the climate of opinion had softened around Bloomsbury. People were beginning to understand that Cézanne was not a madman and that Picasso was not a mountebank. More important still, the whole Victorian conception of sexual morality had been bent. It was not broken. Another war would be needed to accomplish that, but it was severely damaged. The long war against censors and Home Secretaries, in which Bloomsbury was, at that time, very much engaged, was not marked by the victories which we have seen in recent years; but the struggle was engaged upon much more equal terms and with an increasing hope of success. Maynard Keynes, always a political optimist, urged the Liberal Party to make sexual liberty part of its official platform.

Bloomsbury, which had been scattered by the war, diverted into new jobs or isolated in various parts of the country, was reunited. The old state of constant and easy intercourse that had existed before the war could not be re-created so that, to Vanessa Bell, it seemed that Bloomsbury really ended in 1914. But the

The Hogarth Press symbol, 1925

original members had survived the war and they continued to meet. Something that can be called Bloomsbury continued to exist but with a few absentees – less was seen of Sydney Waterlow, Norton and Adrian Stephen; and on the other hand there were a great many new friends, people who were in substantial agreement with Bloomsbury, friends who became almost indistinguishable from the original nucleus.

Success brought imitation. In the arts the young imitator – and this describes nearly all young artists – is likely to follow one of two courses, and whichever he takes is likely to be of disservice to his master. Either he will become a mere shadow of that which he admires and thus serve to give the world a very unfavourable image of his teacher, or he will presently discover his own style and reject, perhaps violently, that which he once admired. Bloomsbury, I think, bred followers of both kinds and certainly the former did much to confuse the scene and to make it hard to know where Bloomsbury began and where it ended.

The Economic Consequences of the Peace was published in 1919, *Vision and Design* in 1920, *Queen Victoria* in 1921, *Night and Day* in 1919 and *Jacob's Room* in 1922. The decade grew up with Bloomsbury in its consciousness. A visitor to the annual exhibitions of the London Group would find the walls covered with essays in the manner of Duncan Grant; a reader of *The Nation* would discover Bloomsbury on every other page. Inevitably there were some who, finding the intellectual climate less congenial and seeing so much critical power concentrated in so few hands, felt that this was a powerful and perhaps unscrupulous admiration society, a society the members of which took care to praise each other's work and to exclude outsiders.

Bloomsbury can be acquitted of such obvious charges. Clive Bell did not praise the paintings of Roger Fry; Virginia Woolf was not particularly kind about Strachey's *Elizabeth and Essex*. T.S. Eliot, the great opponent in literature of Bloomsbury and of all that Bloomsbury stood for, found in Leonard and Virginia Woolf publishers and friends. Young painters, indeed precisely those young painters who were attempting to break away from the influence of Duncan Grant, found immediate and very practical sympathy in Bloomsbury.

Nevertheless I think that the mistrust and dislike of Bloomsbury was very understandable. Success is never, in itself, an endearing quality and in the 1920s Bloomsbury was unforgivably successful. Worse still, success seemed to come by divine right. A large element of Bloomsbury was composed of the heirs of 'aristocratic' families, 'aristocracies' such as those which Virginia Woolf describes in *Night and Day*. The Hilberrys are unsympathetic, despite their virtues, not simply because they have money and privilege but because they assume that they will, in the natural course of things, play a leading role in the cultural life of England. Members of Bloomsbury were accused of arrogance, of intellectual snobbery. But it was worse than that, they did not need to be arrogant; they could afford *not* to be snobbish. They were accused of being exclusive and here again the accusation is both true and false. As I have said, the circle widened enormously during the post-war period, and yet there was at the same time a centripetal force at work. There always had been: the original break with 'good' society, the Post-Impressionist Exhibition, the war, all had a unifying effect, and there was for a time something that might be called an inner circle, an 'old Bloomsbury' composed of those members who had served in the same campaigns, witnessed the same triumphs and endured the same disasters. Between them there was a special relationship, an affinity that can hardly be described in words and now, writing of it, I am not sure to what extent it actually existed, and yet I think that there was something that might be felt – and magnified – by the outsider.

He, the outsider, might well be forgiven, not for entertaining the nightmare fancies of Sir John Rothenstein, but for considering that there was in Bloomsbury a little too much awareness of cultural lineage, a shade of complacency engendered by a softer intellectual climate, a touch of pride.

D.G from D.G.

No. 1 Dec 1920

A Catalogue of secondhand English & Foreign Books

offered for sale by

Birrell & Garnett

19 Taviton St Gordon Sq.

London. W.C.1.

Catalogue no. 1 of Birrell & Garnett's bookshop, 1920

To these charges another and, in a sense, a much more serious accusation might be added. Bloomsbury's ideas had outlived their usefulness almost before they were expressed; they were tragically and radically overtaken by history.

What I call Bloomsbury ideas may be deduced from four publications of the nineteen-twenties: *The Economic Consequences of the Peace* by Maynard Keynes, *Civilisation* by Clive Bell, *Orlando* and *A Room of One's Own* by Virginia Woolf.

The Economic Consequences of the Peace seems to me to contain two arguments, one economic, one moral and political. To a layman the economic argument seems as unanswerable as it did to me when, as a child, Keynes told me that he was going to Versailles to tell the Allies that the Germans could not pay what they had not got. The moral argument is at bottom equally clear. It is certainly immoral to try to establish the hegemony of one's own state when that is precisely the crime of which one has accused one's opponent. But Keynes to some extent clouds the moral issue by his method of attack. Versailles was not a 'Carthaginian' peace in the sense of being a peace that would permanently disable Germany – better perhaps if it had been; it was a peace such as that which the Samnians imposed upon the Romans, who were thereby humiliated but not permanently disarmed. Here indeed the critics of Versailles were on sure ground, for no better formula could have been found for ultimate disaster and, in urging the *wisdom* of magnanimity, Keynes was altogether right.

Keynes's method of attack is very close to that of Strachey, but whereas Strachey deflates the heroes of the Victorian age, Keynes addresses himself to his contemporaries. The great war leaders, Wilson, Clemenceau and, above all, Lloyd George are drastically diminished. The immensity of their task, the grandeur of their opportunity, serve to give proper scale to these stupid, greedy, angry little men, and they appear in the end, not as monsters of wickedness, but as incapable, irresponsible pygmies who, by some fearful mischance, have been allowed to play ball with the world.

The book was written in a hurry: it was a polemic and an angry polemic. It is not my purpose, neither is it within my power, to consider the justice of the argument, but it is interesting to consider the nature of the crimes of which Keynes believes the Allied leaders to have been guilty. They were stupidity and anger. Wilson was plain stupid, Clemenceau plain angry, Lloyd George, for whom Keynes reserves his harshest censures, was clever enough to rise superior to anger and yet stupid enough to let anger be his guide. He, at least, should have known better and yet, for purely demagogic reasons, chose the baser side.

The Economic Consequences of the Peace forms an excellent prologue to Clive Bell's *Civilisation.* For that book, beginning with the statement that we had, supposedly, been fighting for civilisation, proceeds to ask what is civilisation? The question is not very easily answered. And although the author proceeds with great spirit and some wit to say what it is *not*, he ceases to be so convincing when he attempts a positive definition. As Virginia Woolf put it: 'He has great fun in the opening chapters but in the end it turns out that civilisation is a lunch party at No. 50 Gordon Square.'

This criticism, though brief, and of course unfair, contains a good deal of truth. Civilisation is, we are told, a means to good states of mind, that is to say, to those states of mind which the author values; it has nothing to do with social organisation or with technology. The three unquestionably civilised states have been Athens in the fifth century BC, Italy from the mid-fifteenth century to 1527, and France from the Fronde to the Revolution; the nineteenth century is tacitly rejected as barbarous, and so indeed is much else. But in fact the limits are narrower still; it is the great age of French civilisation that really attracts the author, and even here he manages to forget the age of Louis XIV in his passion for that of Louis XV and Louis XVI.

The nostalgic affection for the eighteenth century which Clive Bell shares in common with Lytton Strachey and Virginia Woolf is certainly one that can be defended. It was an interval between the wars of religion and of nationalism, in which tensions between classes were comparatively mild and for which, if one shares Bloomsbury's delight in the cultivation of reason, friendship and the more amiable pleasures, there is much to be said. But as a basis for a definition of civilisation it hardly seems large enough.

42 Duncan Grant's studio at Charleston

43 Roger Fry and Julian Bell playing chess, painted by Vanessa Bell

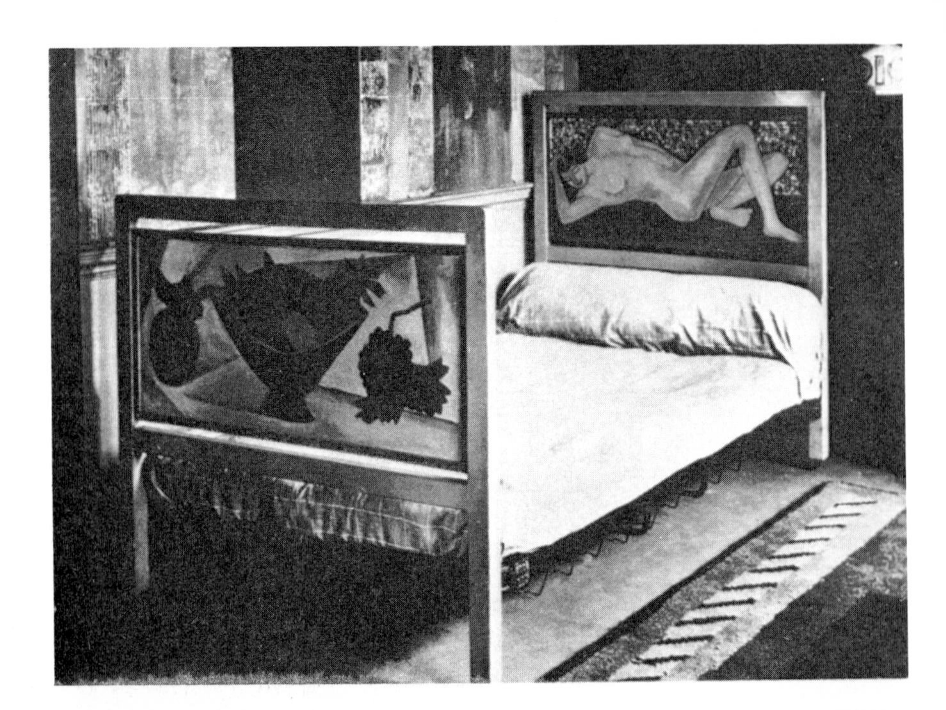

44 Omega Workshop bed, decorated by Roger Fry

45 Omega table and pottery, textile designed by Vanessa Bell

46 Nina Hamnett and Winifred Gill displaying Omega fashions. Miss Gill recalled: 'the cloak Nina is wearing was a sort of oyster-coloured satin painted by Duncan Grant; the skirt I am wearing is simply made up of a length of some rather heavy striped silk. The photograph was made at a press view. Nina and I put on the clothes to show them off better . . . if you look you will see Nina's walking shoes and the collar of my woollen jumper . . . our rather sloppy poses and smiles to order were not of our choice.'

47 Jacket design by Duncan Grant, 1932

In fact 'civilisation' is a term which Clive Bell would not apply even to the culture of one century; it belongs in fact only to what he calls the 'civilised nucleus', or more expressively *La Bonne Société*. It is a matter of good manners and refined pleasures, the decoration of a leisure class, and we must, if it is to survive, accept the existence of a servile population which he believes, somewhat optimistically, may be composed of willing slaves, willing, that is, to devote their lives to the satisfaction of the élite.

Such views are hardly calculated to arouse the enthusiasm of left-wing intellectuals, and during the nineteen-thirties they attracted a good deal of unfavourable comment. To the young socialist of that era the entire tone of the book – the tone of one who is more concerned with the formalities of life than with its essential problems – was highly unsympathetic. It seemed that Clive Bell felt it more important to know how to order a good meal than to know how to lead a good life.

If the tone was unsympathetic, the argument was unsatisfactory. An archaeologist who discovered, beneath the sands of the Gobi desert, the platforms and permanent way of an indubitably fifth-century railway terminus, would claim that he had discovered the remains of a civilisation and all the sane world would agree with him. No one in his senses would say: we cannot tell whether these people were civilised until we know whether they made dirty jokes in the right tone of voice. And yet, this is the implication of Clive Bell's argument. In other words we know and tacitly admit that civilisation depends upon material wealth and material wealth produced cultural phenomena of which the society of Mme du Deffand is but one. It is a thing that is both good and bad in its results, and to look at it from the top only, so to speak, is utterly unrealistic and reactionary.

Thus we argued in the 'thirties, and from this we proceeded to infer that Bloomsbury was, as Mr Moody says, concerned only with the 'civilisation in the mind' and that this concern led to a disastrous political attitude expressed – I am again quoting from Mr Moody – 'mostly in righteous scorn for the barbarian, philistine and populace.'

Here, however, we overlooked some of the evidence, notably a short essay entitled *A Civilised Man* written by Leonard Woolf.

Cover by Vanessa Bell for *The Legend of Monte della Sibilla*, 1923

Woolf's 'civilised man' is Erasmus, and Woolf considers him civilised not because of his rationality and his sense of values, or at least not only on their account, but because of his political attitude. His contemporaries and his biographers have blamed him severely, either because he was critical of Rome at the time of Luther's assault or because he refused to throw in his lot with the reformers, but Woolf sees that Erasmus was opposed to both parties in that both were bigoted, cruel, hateful and unreasonable – in a word that they were both guilty of savagery. To oppose them both was therefore the plain duty of a civilised man.

For Woolf civilisation is something that has never existed but has sometimes been a possibility; it has not existed because to become a reality it would have to exist at every level of society, and for this very reason there have always been elements in the state which, having a vested interest in violence and superstition, have taken very good care that it shall always be aborted.

It will be seen that both Clive Bell and Leonard Woolf are talking about something different from the civilisation of my hypothetical archaeologist. But the difference between them is striking: Clive Bell sees civilisation as something that exists only in an élite and from which the helots who serve that élite are permanently excluded. The manner in which civilisation is to be preserved is immaterial; if it can be maintained by a democracy so much the better, but there is no fundamental objection to a tyranny so long as it maintains a cultured class with unearned incomes. To Leonard Woolf it appears that all attempts to make a civilisation which relies upon military or ecclesiastical power are doomed, for these forces are bound to turn against reason when reason threatens their supremacy; the only hope for civilisation is that it shall find support in the masses.

The difference of approach is of enormous importance; it is the difference between one who would and one who would not submit to fascism. Nevertheless there is some common ground, for while both would in the end accept the use of force, the one in resisting, the other in establishing a tyrant, to both the idea of violence was extremely painful, and painful in part because it implied the abdication of reason.

Here we return to the common feeling of Bloomsbury, one that was certainly shared and in an elliptical fashion expressed by Virginia Woolf.

Orlando, published in 1928, is very much a document of the period; it is the gayest, the most optimistic, of Virginia Woolf's novels. The fantasy is built around Vita Sackville West, a friend and in some respects a 'Bloomsbury' figure. The book is in part a parody of that then fashionable literary form, the fictionalised biography; it leaps away from fact tracing its hero's career from the late sixteenth to the early twentieth century. In the middle of the seventeenth century the hero becomes a woman. In her attitude towards English history, which is a principal theme of the book, Virginia Woolf reflects pretty exactly the attitudes of her time. The sixteenth and seventeenth century are beautiful, wild and fantastic; the nineteenth century is portrayed as a darkening of the heavens, 'a turbulent welter of cloud', a damp, chilly blight, which lifts during the reign of Edward VII; and it is the eighteenth century and her own age – for all its terrors – that she loves best.

But the true importance of *Orlando*, from the point of view of the student of Bloomsbury, only becomes apparent when we consider it in relation to *A Room of One's Own*, published in the following year (1929). This book argues that if a young woman is to learn to write she must have £500 a year and a room of her own. It is important to notice some of Virginia Woolf's reasons for urging the equal treatment of women students. She deplores the disabilities of her sex, not only because they are unjust, but because they engender ugly states of mind. The Pankhurst of literature will 'write in a rage where she should write calmly. She will write foolishly where she should write wisely. She will write of herself where she should write of her characters.'

The authoress discovered this unamiable vein of fury in herself. Musing upon Professor X engaged in writing his monumental work *The Mental, Moral, and Physical Inferiority of the Female Sex*, she conjured up his appearance:

> 'He was not in my picture a man attractive to women. He was heavily built; he had a great jowl; to balance that he had very small eyes; he was very red in the face. His expression sug-

gested that he was labouring under some emotion that made him jab his pen on the paper as if he were killing some noxious insect as he wrote, but even when he had killed it that did not satisfy him; he must go on killing it; and even so, some cause for anger and irritation remained. Could it be his wife, I asked, looking at my picture? Was she in love with a cavalry officer? Was the cavalry officer slim and elegant, and dressed in astrakhan? Had he been laughed at . . .?'

And then the authoress reflects that not only is the professor angry, she too is angry: 'Anger had snatched my pencil while I dreamt.' Her anger had to be 'explained and done with'. But what about his? The anger of the enraged feminist might be odious; but the anger of women, howsoever terrible to themselves, was nothing so dreadful or so dangerous as the anger of men.

The apparatus of violence, of aggression, may take a literary form, and it is in that form, naturally enough, that Virginia Woolf considers it. She examines the aggressively masculine author and his works, she considers his literary copulations:

'And that, I added, aware of the awful nature of the confession, seems somehow dull. Shakespeare's indecency uproots a thousand other things in one's mind, and is far from being dull. But Shakespeare does it for pleasure; Mr A, as the nurses say, does it on purpose. He does it in protest. He is protesting against the equality of the other sex by asserting his own superiority. He is therefore impeded and inhibited and self-conscious . . .'

And then, looking at the older generation, specifically at Galsworthy and Kipling, she discovers that:

'It is not only that they celebrate male virtues, enforce male values and describe the world of men; it is that the emotion with which these books are permeated is to a woman incomprehensible . . . So with Mr Kipling's officers who turn their backs; and his Sowers who sow the Seed; and his Men who are alone with their Work; and the Flag – one blushes at all these capital letters as if one had been caught eavesdropping at some purely masculine orgy.'

Woodcut by Vanessa Bell from *Monday or Tuesday* (Virginia Woolf), 1921

Virginia Woolf was not unaware of the menace that lay behind this highly masculine and aggressive conception of life and literature:

> 'I began to envisage an age to come of pure, of self-assertive virility, such as the letters of professors (take Sir Walter Raleigh's letters, for instance) seem to forebode, and the rulers of Italy have already brought into being. For one can hardly fail to be impressed in Rome by the sense of unmitigated masculinity . . . Poetry ought to have a mother as well as a father. The fascist poem, one may fear, will be a horrid little abortion such as one sees in a glass jar in the museum of some county town.'

The fault as she sees it lies not with men only but with both sexes. The fatal thing for an artist is to insist upon his sex, and the great writers, such as Shakespeare, Keats, Sterne, Cowper, Lamb, Coleridge and Proust, are in fact androgynous; the female element lives with the male and both are harnessed to the muse.

If now we return to *Orlando*, we shall find the same idea applied not simply to the practice of literature but to the conduct of life. Orlando, having become a woman at the age of thirty, reflects upon her new condition and concludes that:

'"... [it is better] to be clothed with poverty and ignorance, which are the dark garments of the female sex; better to leave the rule and discipline of the world to others; better be quit of martial ambition, the love of power, and all the other manly desires if so one can more fully enjoy the most exalted raptures known to the human spirit, which are," she said aloud, as her habit was when deeply moved, "contemplation, solitude, love."

'"Praise God that I'm a woman!" she cried, and was about to run into the extreme folly – than which none is more distressing in woman or man either – of being proud of her sex, when she paused over the singular word, which, for all we can do to put it in its place, has crept in at the end of the last sentence: "Love."'

And in fact within the terms not only of her fantasy but also I think of real life, Virginia Woolf imagines a solution of human affairs based upon androgynous affections. Orlando's purely virile affection for his intensely feminine Sacha ends in despair and disillusion; but when as a woman she discovers that she is in love with Shelmerdine it is with the exclamation: 'You're a woman, Shel!' to which he responds: 'You're a man, Orlando!', and it is through that nice equation of the sexes that human beings may perhaps come to terms with their passions.

Needless to say these meditations upon aggression and affection had no effect upon the world of practical politics. That world was soon to be left to the management of Mussolini, his pupils and his opposite numbers.

I have reached a point in this more or less chronological survey at which the difficulties to which I alluded in the opening pages of this essay become unavoidable. I knew Bloomsbury at the time of its apogee and disintegration and it seems proper that I should give an eye-witness account of it. I am perplexed by the difficulties of such a task.

Bloomsbury in the 'twenties was, in a material sense, successful. We and our friends began to accumulate luxuries; sometimes there was wine for dinner, there was a motor-car, a new gramophone, a refrigerator, a villa in the South of France. These were not grandly luxurious acquisitions: the wine was not expensive, the car was second-hand, the villa was shared and it was not on the Côte d'Azur. Keynes was the only one to accumulate a fortune; the others were simply becoming 'comfortably off'. Some of the group established connections with the 'beau monde', the world of Lady Colefax and Lady Cunard, the world that Harold Nicolson describes in his diaries, but there were others, particularly the painters, who fought shy of it. 'Old Bloomsbury', as Vanessa Bell called it, and in the late nineteen-twenties and early nineteen-thirties this meant herself and Clive Bell, Leonard and Virginia Woolf, Lytton Strachey, Roger Fry and Duncan Grant, Maynard Keynes and the Desmond MacCarthys, was certainly not *chic*; it was very tolerant in matters of dress, it dined well but without any kind of display. 'Comfortable' is the epithet that seems to me most appropriate.

There was the aesthetic comfort of Sussex gardens full of flowers in which plaster-casts from the antique slowly disintegrated from year to year; high studios that were also living-rooms in which were painted decorations of a kind that would now be considered dreadfully fussy and old-fashioned; rooms made for ease rather than for show, on the walls of which hung the spoils of more adventurous years, *fauve* and cubist pictures that had been purchased when such things could be bought for a few pounds and which were later (alas) used to stave off financial disaster; Negro and Chinese sculpture, tiled tables and cottons made for the African trade, shabby comfortable furniture, big Spanish or Italian pots purchased for ridiculous sums and transported with much labour and anxiety in third-class railway carriages across Europe (and in these, the vast baroque leaves and flowers of the globe artichoke), books in perpetual disorder, a gramophone with a horn like a great arum lily and records of composers from Monteverdi to Beethoven (the nineteenth century was less well represented).

In these rather shabby, but very easy surroundings, the members of Bloomsbury gathered to eat and talk. I don't think that they needed much else to amuse them. Occasionally they might

Illustration by Duncan Grant from *The Legend of Monte della Sibilla*, 1923

listen to the gramophone, play chess, or some outdoor games; playing cards were for children, and so too were most party games. But the pleasures of conversation were sufficient and conversation might lead anywhere, anywhere – in theory at all events – for in these years Bloomsbury was by modern standards rather chaste, so that although it was as willing to discuss buggery as it was to discuss Boethius, and although the atmosphere was completely permissive and tolerant, it was not fond of what Clive Bell would have called *les gros mots* but preferred, perhaps in deference to its children, an elliptical, an indirect mode of discussing the cruder realities of sex.

I think that Bloomsbury's tolerance was tried fairly high by the younger generation. For we had no hesitation – and that in itself is significant – in telling Old Bloomsbury that it had taken the wrong turning, that it had entirely misjudged the social and political situation before 1914, that it ought to have foreseen the war and that its attitude then had been purely negative. Furthermore we pointed out that it had allowed Post-Impressionism to degenerate into something wholly frivolous and fashionable, that it acquiesced in a social system which it knew to be wrong and allowed itself to become a part of the Establishment. Finally that it failed altogether to see that the one hope of the world, despite all its errors and despite all the civilised squeamishness that it might provoke, was Soviet Russia. Such, very roughly, and with great differences of individual position, was the case that we made against Bloomsbury, and it was argued with increasing tension as the drama of the 'thirties developed. Bloomsbury was always ready to listen to such opinions and to debate them fairly.

This last paragraph has carried me beyond the 'twenties and into a period in which Bloomsbury was but a shadow of its former self, even though some of its members still had important tasks to accomplish. The deaths of Lytton Strachey in 1931 and of Roger Fry in 1934 altogether changed the character of the group. The events of the 'thirties left it without any common doctrine or attitude. As I have said, the nineteen-twenties made it and broke it; it was then that it soared, burst in lazy scintillating splendour and slowly expired in still glowing fragments.

5
The Character of Bloomsbury

I imagine that I have said enough to give the reader a fair idea of what I believe to be Bloomsbury's main characteristics. Before attempting to tie my arguments together in what I hope may be a reasonably tidy knot I would like once more to emphasise the fact that I am writing about something almost impalpable, almost indefinable.

Imagine a great highway up which walks a heterogeneous crowd – the British Intellectuals. There is in that great concourse a little group of people who talk eagerly together, it is but one of many similar groups and sometimes groups seem to merge. Figures move in towards the centre and move away again to walk elsewhere; some are silent, some are loquacious. When the great ambling procession begins to march in time to a military band, the part to which we devote our attention falls out of step; this makes it, for a time, conspicuous, and yet even so it is not perfectly definable. There are other groups which also become noticeably civilian; moreover, martial music is an infectious thing, and it is hard to say who is and who is not walking to its rhythms. Then, at a later stage, the group suddenly becomes enlarged. Everyone seems to be joining it, so that it is no longer a group, it has become a crowd. It dissolves, the original members disappear, and it is gone.

The image is sufficiently banal but I can find none better to convey the amorphous character of my subject.

What then had this group in common apart from the fact that it was talking? Perhaps this in itself may be a distinction, for there are groups that do not talk, they shout and yell and come to blows. Bloomsbury did none of these things. Despite tremendous differences of opinion, it talked. Indeed it did more, it talked on the whole reasonably, it talked as friends may talk together, with all the licence and all the affection of friendship. It believed, in fact, in pacific and rational discussion.

Now there is nothing remarkable about this; most of us behave quietly and carry on rational conversations. But we also do other things: we create works of art and perform acts of worship, we make love and we make war, we yell and we come to blows.

Bloomsbury sometimes did these things, too, and in fact we all live our lives upon two contradictory principles, that of reason and that of unreason. We come, as best we may, to a synthesis of opposites; the peculiar thing about Bloomsbury was the nature of its dialectic.

A creative artist in modern society can hardly be unaware of the charms of unreason. He is, by the nature of his employment, so very much more dependent upon intuition than upon ratiocination. Art in our time – I am thinking of the visual arts in particular – has broken free from any pretence of utility. The artist is bound by no rational programme, no reasonable dependence upon mimesis; his images are made in accordance with unbiddable inner necessities, they are such stuff as dreams are made on and are judged in accordance with an aesthetic which is of its nature dogmatic and impervious to reason. While this is obviously true of the musical and visual arts, in literature, where a certain tincture of thought may be apprehended, the sway of the unreasoning emotions, the 'thinking in the blood' that makes for heroism, passion, chastity, and nearly all the strong emotions that are the very stuff of tragedy, can be overwhelmingly powerful.

The irrational has an even stronger pull, in that it is so often a communal phenomenon. He who thinks much is perforce a lonely man, whereas the great unreasoning emotions of mankind bring us into a glorious brotherhood with our kind. We feel (I quote from Wyndham Lewis) 'the love and understanding of blood brothers, of one culture, children of the same traditions, whose deepest social interests, when all is said and done, are one: that is the only sane and realistic journey in the midst of a disintegrating world. That, as I interpret it, is the national socialist doctrine of *Blutsgefühl.*'[16]

These words were written at a time when it was still possible for a partial observer to ignore the uglier side of National

Socialism. They may serve to remind us that the Janus-face of Social Love is Social Hatred; it is hard to create a God without also creating a Devil.

In the year 1900 the world had not seen what a modern nation could do when it put its trust in *Blutsgefühl*, but it was obvious enough that if men were to surrender to the voice of authority, to yield to the strong irrational demands of religion, or nationalism, or sexual superstition, hatred no less than love would be the result. The hatred of Christian for Christian, of nation for nation, the blind unreasoning hatred that had hounded Oscar Wilde or killed Socrates, these were all communal emotions that resulted from irrationality. The sleep of reason engenders monsters, the monsters of violence. It was therefore absolutely necessary, if charity were to survive in the world, that reason should be continually awake.

This I think was the assumption that determined Bloomsbury's attitude and gave a distinctive tone to its art and to its conversation. No one today could for one moment suppose that the irrational forces in life, the love of death and of violence, were not present in the world, or that they do not lie somewhere within each of us, but whereas to some of us they are not merely immanent but something to be embraced and accepted with joy, connected as they are with so many great spiritual experiences, for Bloomsbury they were something to be chained, muzzled and as far as possible suppressed. The great interest of Bloomsbury lies in the consistency, the thoroughness and, despite almost impossible difficulties, the success with which this was done.

The first great step was to transfer nineteenth-century scepticism from the cosmic to the personal field. The rejection of dogmatic morality meant that the traditional sanctions of social hatred were removed. G. E. Moore's limpid intellectual honesty remained and with it a morality which excluded, or very nearly excluded, aggressive violence. As Maynard Keynes says:

> 'The New Testament is a handbook for politicians compared with the unworldliness of Moore's chapter on the "Ideal". Indeed there is, in *Principia Ethica*, a certain remoteness from the hurly-burly of everyday life, which, I suspect, results from

the extraordinarily sheltered and optimistic society that was to be found in Cambridge at the beginning of the century, and this mild emotional climate was, I apprehend, an indispensable prerequisite for a society which attempted to lead a completely non-aggressive existence.'

'We repudiated' – I am again quoting from Maynard Keynes – 'all versions of the doctrine of original sin, of there being insane and irrational springs of wickedness in most men.' Now this may be true, but if it is true it is surprising. It may be true, because the human mind is capable of such extraordinary feats of inconsistency, but if one considers the novels of E. M. Forster, which are deeply involved in this very question, I find it hard to believe that his contemporaries completely ignored the menace of the irrational.

Death and violence walk hand in hand through these novels; the goblins walk over the universe and although they are driven away, we know that they are still there; children are killed, young men are struck down with swords, blind hatred and blind prejudice are never far away. Where Forster differs from his friends and is not, to my mind, altogether Bloomsbury, is in his essentially reverent and optimistic attitude. His reverence is, to be sure, evasive and half veiled. But it is there all right, in the woods of Hertfordshire or the caves of Marabar; there is something that escapes his reasoning and I can just imagine him buying a rather small dim candle to burn before the altar of some rather unpopular saint – something that Lytton Strachey, for instance, could never have done.

Ethically however he seems to me altogether on the same side as Bloomsbury: conscious, deeply conscious of the dark irrational side of life but absolutely convinced of the necessity of holding fast to reason, charity and good sense.

Bloomsbury may or may not have appreciated the role of 'the insane and irrational springs of wickedness' that seem so close to the surface of life in *Howard's End*, but must it not have seen them gushing forth in cascades of derisive laughter or in torrents of abuse in the Grafton Gallery Exhibition?

The public reaction to Gauguin, Cézanne and van Gogh was

'Interior' from *Twelve Original Woodcuts* by Roger Fry, 1921

not founded upon any process of reasoning. The public laughed or was angry because it did not understand, and also, I think, because it *did* understand. People could hardly have been so angry, would hardly have reiterated, again and again, the charge of indecency (this hardly seems credible when we think of Cézanne's still lives) or of anarchism, unless they had become aware of some profoundly disturbing, some quite positive emotion in that which they so much hated and were later, with equal unreason, so greatly to love.

Now at first sight it would appear that when faced by such obstinate and furious aesthetic convictions reason would be powerless, and indeed speechless. Speechless she was not. Both Clive Bell and Roger Fry had plenty to say about art between 1910 and 1914. They would most willingly argue with anyone who would listen to them, and while Clive Bell elaborated his theory of significant form, Roger Fry was explaining, persuading, reasoning in talk and conversation, and in letters to the press. Here, Fry seems to be arguing a purely intellectual case. His method is to find common ground and then proceed by a process of enquiry: We both agree in liking A but you do not like B.

What then is the difference between A and B? It turns out of course to be something very insubstantial and the opponent is in a perfectly nice and entirely rational way flattered. Such is the method of his argument: he refuses to be dogmatic and he refuses to be angry. He appeals continually to reason.

There was a certain element of deception here, not, I think, of conscious deception. Up to a point Roger Fry's arguments were fair enough, but at a certain point a mixture of charm and what, for lack of a better word I would call 'overwhelmingness' would clinch the victory. His friends knew this to their cost, for when Roger started some really March hare, some business of black boxes, dark stars, thaumaturgic parascientific nonsense for which he had a strong though inconsistent affection, his force of character, his air of sweet reasonableness and scientific integrity, was such that he could convince himself and his friends of the truth of whatever chimerical bee might for the moment have flown into his bonnet.

The excellence of Seurat, Cézanne and Poussin were not, in my opinion at all events, chimerical nonsense, but Fry made his hearers believe in those excellencies, made them feel them by means of a method of argument which had the purest air of scientific objectivity, in a field in which, ultimately, science has no authority. Roger Fry is concerned not only to present a 'fair argument' but to argue about fair things. By this I mean that he does not readily allude to the esoteric or mysterious side of art but talks rather about sensual and easily demonstrable characteristics. His attitude to primitive art is revealing: confronted by Negro sculpture he is amazed by its plastic freedom, its 'three-dimensionalness', the intelligence with which the negro translates the forms of nature, his exquisite taste in the handling of material. Only in one brief allusive phrase does he touch on the magical purposes of these articles. Compare this with the attitude of Emil Nolde, as reported by his latest biographer:

> 'He saw in this art, with its abstract and rhythmic sense of ornament and color and its mystic power, an affirmation of his own anti-classical art. He was one of the first artists to protest against the relegation of primitive art objects to anthropological

48 Leonard Woolf (and his dog Sally) at Monks House, by Vanessa Bell, 1939

49 Vanessa Bell at Charleston, 1960

50 Duncan Grant at Charleston, 1977

51 *Significant Form* by Max Beerbohm
'Mr. Clive Bell: I always think that when one feels one's been carrying a theory too far, then's the time to carry it a little further.'
'Mr. Roger Fry: A little? Good heavens man! Are you growing old?'
The term 'significant form' was used by Clive Bell in his book, *Art*, published in February 1914.

museums, where they were still exhibited as scientific specimens. His own "blood and soil" mystique made him an early proponent of the indigenous art of all peoples.'[17]

'Dessert' from *Twelve Original Woodcuts* by Roger Fry, 1921

In fact, of course, the tendency of the Bloomsbury art critics was to look away from content altogether. It is a tendency better exemplified by Clive Bell than by Roger Fry; neither of them in fact held it with complete consistency. But undoubtedly the main tendency of their writings between, say, 1910 and 1925 is in the direction of a purely formalist attitude. The aesthetic emotion is, or at least can be and probably should be, something of almost virgin purity, a matter of harmonious relationships, of calculated patterning, entirely removed from the emotive feelings; and these, when they do occur in works of art, are not only irrelevant and 'literary' but productive of that vulgarity, sentimentality and rhetoric which is the besetting sin of nineteenth-century art. Indeed it is the existence of that kind of 'Salon Art' which, I fancy, prompted these rather hazardous generalisations. The sentimentality of Raphael and Correggio, the violence of Goya and Breughel, are not reproved but dismissed as irrelevant, or at least inessential.

Something of the same attitude may, I think, be traced in the actual paintings of the group. Bloomsbury finds its masters amongst the Apollonian rather than the Dionysiac painters, turning to Piero della Francesca rather than Michelangelo, Poussin rather than Bernini, Constable rather than Turner. Amongst the Post-Impressionists it looks to van Gogh and to Gauguin but above all to Cézanne.

Cézanne, whose genius is large enough to be interpreted in many ways, is used as a guide to architectonic solidity, to the careful ordering and redisposition of nature. He is not used as the Vorticists and the Germans use him, as a provider of anguished angularities, violent, emphatic, exclamatory drawing and dynamic chaos.

The insistence that art be removed from life, that painting should aspire to the condition of music, which may certainly be deduced from the writings of Clive Bell and Roger Fry, would, one might have thought, have been translated in practice into pure abstraction, but apart from a few brief essays made before 1914 Bloomsbury painting remains anchored to the visible world. For this there was an important psychological reason: the Bloomsbury painters were, I think, intensely interested in content.

Dustjacket for *The Moment*, design by Vanessa Bell, Hogarth Press, 1947

Vanessa Bell continued to the last to paint landscapes and still lives, girls, children and flowers, which to me at all events seem to be replete with psychological interest, while at the same time firmly denying that the story of a picture had any importance whatsoever. Duncan Grant has always been rather less positive in his statements; his lyrical inventions are equally if not more suggestive of a highly literary mood. And the mood, which may also be observed in the work of Roger Fry, is again one of passion firmly controlled by reason, sensual enjoyment regulated by the needs of serenity.

Looking at Duncan Grant's *Lemon Gatherers* in the Tate and considering its quietly lyrical quality, the calm precision of its design, its tacit sensuality, who could doubt that in 1914 he would be a conscientious objector? The answer of course is that anyone could doubt it and that paintings do not have such clear diagnostic value as that, but I let the sentence stand because, overstatement though it is, it conveys a certain measure of truth. Bloomsbury painting, like Bloomsbury writing and Bloomsbury politics, is pacific even when it is not pacifist. It is by no means unconscious of violence, but it reacts against it either by deliberately avoiding it, or by criticism and mockery, or by trying to find a formula to contain it.

On the whole the painters shrink from violence. Roger Fry attempts to explain art in other terms; for him violence was something stupid and irrational, a means to pain when clearly pleasure is the end of life. Lytton Strachey and Maynard Keynes both fight it with ridicule, Clive Bell veers between ridicule and evasion, Virginia Woolf finds its origin in the relationship of the sexes and seeks its cure in their fusion. All turn to reason as the one possible guide in human affairs precisely because the forces of violence lie within even the best-intentioned men. As Clive Bell wrote, 'those were not naturally cruel men who burnt heretics for not agreeing with them, and witches for being vaguely disquieting, they were simply men who refused to submit prejudice to reason.'[18]

Even those who would declare that faith is in some sort a higher thing than reason would, probably, agree that there is a good deal to be said for this view – in theory. The difficulty, as

From the title-page of *Original Woodcuts by Various Artists*, incorporating the Omega Motif, 1918

anyone who surveys the world from Birmingham, Alabama to Salisbury, Rhodesia, and back again by way of Saigon, will know is that when it comes to a struggle between reason and violence reason nearly always takes a beating.

And yet this is not the whole picture. Reason does win victories and Bloomsbury has helped to win them. This paradoxically is one of the things that makes us undervalue its achievements. It would be quite easy to compile an anthology of Bloomsbury's pronouncements on prudery, sexual persecution and censorship, which would command the assent of nearly all literate people at the present day and would, for that reason, be rather dull; the audacities of one age become the platitudes of the next.

But in its larger effort, the effort to live a life of rational and pacific freedom, to sacrifice the heroic virtues in order to avoid the heroic vices, Bloomsbury was attempting something which, to the next generation, seemed unthinkable. It could only have been thought of by people in a favoured social position at a particularly favourable moment in the history of England. It could be maintained, but only just maintained, between the years 1914 and 1918 because in that war it was still possible for an intelligent man or woman to be neutral. The advocates of reason, tolerance and scepticism frequently found themselves confronted by individuals who were partly or wholly on the other side. I have mentioned Fitzjames Stephen and his generation, D. H. Lawrence, Wyndham Lewis and Rupert Brooke – a very heterogeneous collection of talents, but all united in their belief that at a certain point emotion, not reason, must be our guide, and that heroic violence is more desirable than unheroic calm. But with all of these, as also with a belligerent England, some kind of parley, some kind of communication was possible; between them and Bloomsbury there was not a complete polarity of views. With the advent of Fascism, Bloomsbury was confronted by a quarrel in which, believing what they believed, neutrality was impossible. The old pacifism had become irrelevant and the group as a group ceased to exist.

Notes

1 A. D. Moody, *Virginia Woolf*, 1963. p. 5.
2 John Jewkes, *Ordeal by Planning*, 1948. p. 28.
3 John Rothenstein, *Modern English Painters, Lewis to Moore*, 1956. p. 14.
4 See F. W. Maitland, *The Life and Letters of Leslie Stephen*, 1906. p. 144; and Leslie Stephen, *The Life of Fitzjames Stephen*, 1895. pp. 230–1, 317, 326 *et passim*.
5 Noël Annan, *Leslie Stephen*, 1948. pp. 99–101.
6 *Letters of Lady Anne Thackeray Ritchie*, Ed. Hester Ritchie. I am indebted to Mrs L. D. Ettlinger for calling my attention to the importance of Lady Ritchie's influence.
7 Stephen Chaplin and Quentin Bell, 'The Ideal Home Rumpus' in *Apollo* LXXX No. 32. See also Michel, 'Tyros and Portraits', *ibid* LXXXII No. 42, and correspondence in LXXXIII No. 47.
8 E. M. Forster, Goldsworthy *Lowes Dickinson*, 1934. p. 162.
9 H. G. Wells, *War and the Future*, 1917. pp. 203–5.
10 Christopher Hassall, *Rupert Brooke*, 1965. pp. 362, 364, 442, and 460.
11 Frieda Lawrence, *Not I, But the Wind*, 1935. pp. 77–8. I am indebted to Mrs Beata Duncan who called my attention to this passage.
12 See *Letters of D. H. Lawrence*, Ed. Harry T. Moore, 1962. Vol. I; Frieda Lawrence, *Memoirs and Correspondence*, Ed. Tedlock, 1961; Nehl, *D. H. Lawrence – a Composite Biography*, 1957; Garnett, *Flowers of the Forest*, 1955; Keynes, *Two Memoirs*, 1949; and Leavis, 'Keynes, Lawrence and Cambridge' in *The Common Pursuit*, 1952. The curious reader will discover that I also accepted Keynes's account of the matter in *Bloomsbury and the Fine Arts*, in *Leeds Art Calendar*, No. 55, 1964. It should be said that Mr David

Garnett, who has seen this work in manuscript, remains completely unconvinced by my arguments.

13 Leonard Woolf, *Sowing*, 1961. pp. 153–4.
14 Adrian Stephen, *The Dreadnought Hoax*, 1936. pp. 10–11.
15 Virginia Woolf, *Roger Fry*, 1940. p. 186.
16 Wyndham Lewis, *Hitler*, 1931. p. 109.
17 Roger Fry, *Negro Sculpture*, 1920; repr. in *Vision and Design*, 1920; and Peter Selz, *Emil Nolde*, 1963. p. 33.
18 Clive Bell, *On British Freedom*, 1923. p. 47.

Illustrations

Line illustrations in the text

Index

Corrigenda

This edition exactly follows the first edition. These notes may serve to correct certain errors and bring the text up to date.

page 16 'David Garnett ... Leonard Woolf ... ' The former died in 1981, the latter in 1969.

27 'The Mausoleum Book' has been published with an introduction by Alan Bell (Clarendon Press, 1977).

50 'Roger Fry ... sometime director of the Metropolitan Museum' – in fact Curator.

54 'Duncan Grant to lunch at Durbins ... to meet some dealers' – actually he went there not to meet dealers but to paint Pamela Fry's portrait. She was set in a most agonising pose. (Pamela Fry is now Pamela Diamand.)

100 'decorations of a kind that would now be considered dreadfully fussy ...' – 'now' = 1967.

114 'a few brief essays made before 1914' – more recent scholarship has shown that this is an understatement.

117 'Rhodesia, and back by way of Saigon' – no longer topical but still true.